DEFINITIONS

ESSAYS IN CONTEMPORARY CRITICISM

Second Series

DEFINITIONS

ESSAYS IN CONTEMPORARY CRITICISM

Second Series

BY

HENRY SEIDEL CANBY, Ph.D.

Editor of *The Saturday Review of Literature*
Lecturer in English in Yale University

KENNIKAT PRESS, INC./PORT WASHINGTON, N. Y.

DEFINITIONS

Series One: Copyright 1922 by Harcourt, Brace and World, Inc.
Copyright 1950 by Henry S. Canby
Reissued in 1967 by Kennikat Press by arrangement with
Harcourt, Brace and World, Inc.

Series Two: Copyright 1924 by Harcourt, Brace and World, Inc.
Copyright 1952 by Henry S. Canby
Reissued in 1967 by Kennikat Press by arrangement with
Harcourt, Brace and World, Inc.

Library of Congress Catalog Card No: 67-27582

Manufactured in the United States of America

Analyzed in the ESSAY & GENERAL LITERATURE INDEX

Acknowledgments

The author wishes to acknowledge the courtesy of *The Century Magazine, The Encyclopedia Britannica Company,* and *The Literary Review* of *The New York Evening Post* for permission to reprint such of these essays as have been first published by them.

Acknowledgements

Preface

"Definitions," First Series, was an attempt to explain the course of contemporary literature by the informal instead of the formal method. It is always easy to state some theory of criticism and then proceed to whack about among contemporaries with it; but the honester method is to look at movements, tendencies, books, and try to understand them before reaching conclusions.

"Definitions," First Series, was a book of, not on, criticism. The stream of literature is as unceasing as the stream of life, and "Definitions," Second Series, is merely the result of two years' more living. It contains perhaps more brief essays upon tendencies, prejudices, perplexities, and absurdities in literature, but the complexion of this book is much the same as the other, its critical attitude (so much more important sometimes than formulated theory) is, the author believes, not different, and if different (so he hopes), wiser. It reflects the vigorous, turbulent, successful years of 1922, '23, and '24 in literature, but draws upon a wider range of thought and experience than these dates would indicate.

New Haven, May, 1924.

Contents

x   *Contents*

I

Literature To-day

The Age of Experiment

THERE is such a thing as being too successful. The anthropologists are saying that progress upward is due to superior adaptiveness, from which one might conclude that the more speedily we adapt ourselves to whatever comes along, and the more readily we readapt ourselves when necessary, the better humans we are certain to be. By this reasoning the Harkness Memorial Quadrangle at Yale is a supreme example of adaptiveness in that men, accustomed to live under steel and wood and beneath buildings that shoot upward, borrow wholesale a medieval style created for an utterly different civilization, and adapt their quite unclerical lives to its soothing amenities.

The process is quite the same in religion and quite the same in literature. A violent eclecticism is the most striking characteristic of English literature to-day. I have stood before shelves of freshly published books in an editorial office and tried to think of some principle of resemblance which would run, even faintly, through them all. Such a thread would have been traceable surely in Shakespeare's day, or Pope's. But neither style nor subject nor, apparently, point of view nor genre nor mood nor any of the lighter resemblances seemed to carry through. What possible unifying word can you apply to such a collection except "modern" or "eclectic"?   And what does "modern" mean?

There is a common denominator, however, into which most will divide, and it is to be found, as always, in the undercurrents of belief and interest which flow through a civilization, touching all whom that civilization touches.   It is needless to labor proof that the nature of books is determined by the flow of interest.   Such terms as "the Greek mind" or "the medieval mind" would otherwise possess not even the general meaning which we assign to them.   There is a direct relation between Greek tragedy and Greek philosophy, and there is an open conduit between the mood of the Renaissance and the works of the Renaissance in politics, science, theology, and art.   There is a direct connection, too, between the extravagant eclecticism of modern literature and the medley of philosophies to the tune of which modern civilization marches.   But this is just to say that our books are eclectic because we are eclectic, which does not explain what moderns mean by "modern."

I think that the essential meaning of this term "modern" is to be found in the kind of interest it expresses.   The line of interest to-day falls without, and not within, us.   Our modern interest is characteristically held by circumstances outside of the ego and beyond its past experience, even when we seem to bend our investigation inward and backward.   It is an interest in experiment.   If this is true, and although "outside" and "inside" are wobbly terms which may fail me, I believe it can be proved to be approximately true, then there are corollaries which may help to clear a mind confused by the shouting over what we ought to think and ought not to think of "the trend of literature." Such aid to the doubtful, and not prophecy, is the first duty of criticism.

Take half a dozen characteristic books of recent years. Even if science be left out, this common factor of interest in experiment leaps to the eye. Strachey's "Eminent Victorians" and his "Queen Victoria" were based, for example, upon no new theory of biography so far as I can see to make them "modern," but sprang from a formula: "let us test what we know of these eminent people by new sets of facts, the idea being that we never know what people were until we have tried them by what they did." "Babbitt" and "Main Street," regarded as social documents, were studies in the effect of environment upon human character. "Spoon River Anthology," to go further back for a very illuminating example, is the natural history of a small town, microscopically studied in all possible positions upon the slide.

We must go behind the books to get the whole story. The history of the last half-century is woven through by it. We rest upon the world prevailingly now instead of upon ourselves. Our confidence in the alleged conquest of nature has grown until reliance has become a habit. To read with any penetration, let us say, Thoreau or Emerson has become almost such an experience as to study the Greek classics. We view a different spiritual world and impulses almost contradictory to ours. Within and within these men are always beckoning, even when engrossed by external fact. Evolution fascinates them because it seems to indicate what man can do for his spiritual self. Evolution for us is a guiding theory in our attempt to fit the body to its environment and subdue that environment. They attempt a unity of the personality in the presence of the universe; we court the disunity of never ending experiment.

As a result, a slow swinging away from discipline and self-restraint as the major ideals of Western civilization has been under way for at least a century. The change came first in our advisers and then in us. Instead of urging us to school our ego until it bowed to circumstance, they plead with us to control circumstance. Instead of "be good," they began to say, "Will what is desirable; *go get it.*" They accepted, often unconsciously, the theory that man, being an organism in development, *push,* not *pull,* was what he needed. Ulysses, who would "sail beyond the sunset," Henley, whose head was "bloody, but unbowed," Tennyson, who begged us to rise on our dead selves, were spokesmen. It was felt, and the feeling spreads through our later literature, that experiment, energetically conducted, would lead us anywhere.

The times favored an optimistic theory. It has been said that the prosperity of eighteenth-century New England broke the power of puritan Calvinism. You simply could not believe in such extensive damnation among the dairy meadows of Connecticut or in the bustling streets of Boston. Our times, even if the War be left aside, have been no golden age, but every class has improved its condition in the course of a century, and the favored persons have been more favored by peace and plenty than since the Augustan age.

Restraint—spiritual, mental, physical—relaxed, lost first of all its absurdities, and then its sense of inevitable rightness. It would be interesting to place in descending steps a series of famous stories, from "Rasselas" through "Adam Bede" and "Jude the Obscure" to Sherwood Anderson and Scott Fitzgerald. The reader who took them in order could scarcely escape feeling a changing world, and a new conception of must and ought.

But it was not merely optimism. The fear of God bred melancholy in the Puritan, the fear of dropping behind in the race of evolution makes the modern uneasy and irritable. He feels he must expand with an expanding world. Since we progress by experiment, he feels that he must experiment himself. He must try everything, as the cant phrase goes, at least once. He must look through that arch of experience which Tennyson describes—Tennyson who felt all the impulses to doubt and to break free and to experiment which the young rebels who despise him have adopted as their rule of life. Hence the fear of suppression which appears in so much modern literature and finds its scientific analysis in Jung and Freud. Suppression is the death of experiment. The hero of the earlier books was youth resisting sexual philandering or repenting when temptation led astray. The hero of the modern novel is youth, male or female, who has had experience, whatever the nature or cost. Success or failure is beside the point; experience in itself is a justification for writing the story.

I am not, so far, writing a sermon, and intend to avoid sermonizing. I am not attacking experiment, for experiment has made my age, which has, according to my way of thinking, more good than ill in it. Yet it is undeniable that in our literature, which is the sublimation of our experience, experiment has swallowed discipline and restraint by gulps and is beginning to bite upon purpose. Is there any ultimate purpose in the most modern of modern literature except experiment? You will answer that since life is complex and requires analysis and refinement before it can be understood, to experiment is a sufficient purpose. That has been the idea of many students of the natural sciences, the training-ground of the prophets of our generation. They have regarded observation and discovery as ends in themselves, expecting vaguely that their successors would pick up the pieces and make something coherent out of them. As a result, although, thanks to the vast number of new facts ready to work with, the advance of scientific knowledge has been great, the wastage of effort has been phenomenal, and the results, as the War proved, far less valuable than we had hoped. It was the idea also of scientific scholarship, and literary shelves have been stacked with texts now seen to be quite useless. A lack of any purpose in much of this scholarship except crudely to collect facts by experiment has been mournfully evident to all who have had reason to know.

And so, less perhaps, but not otherwise, it has been with so-called creative literature. In due measure, experiment is the soul of creation, but in excess it is its mete and bound. The realists like Zola, who trod eagerly upon the heels of nineteenth-century science, fuddled themselves with experiment. Their novels, like the books of the new school of American realists, were crowded with fact and minute description, never organized into lucid significance. We agree now that artistically they failed, even as we shall admit that the experimental pictures of Mid-Western life now current will have their chief value in the future as materials for social history. Look for "Main Street" in 1955 on the shelves devoted to the background of American history. The psycho-fictionists also, Miss Sinclair for an example, how clearly does she lean in "Anne Severn and the Fieldings" upon studies of man's psychology, how desirous she is to contribute her experiment! And H. G. Wells, might not his novels be the publications of a very human laboratory for social, moral, and mental research? Is he not now as much a research student (with an artist's technique) as when in his youth he practised biology in the University of London!

"Wait and see" is the text which might be printed at the head of all this modern literature, in which much

lyric poetry and the majority of critical essays and
most serious plays are to be included. "Wait and
see," says Bernard Shaw, "how the social forces I display will remold society." "Wait and see," says D.
H. Lawrence, "what will come of the sex instinct when
suppressed or set loose in man." "Wait and see," says
Miss Virginia Woolf, "what you will make of people
viewed as I view them." "Wait and see," say the
writers of a thousand American short stories, "what
boys and girls will do if you give them love and
wealth." The leaning is, you observe, all outward,
upon circumstance. We are to proceed by the results
of experiment, and therefore must expand and expand
into wider experience before we can go on and up. It
is the diametric opposite of the eremite's formula.

There can be, of course, no standards in this literature except the purely esthetic, for there can be no
standards in literary experiment except successful expression. You cannot demand a thesis, a solution, or
even a coherent meaning in experiment. This may
satisfy the determined artist and those disciples of
Croce who wish to disregard substance in literature,
but many will remain dissatisfied. If the critic's analysis reads, "This book is a partial view, it is abnormal
[or immoral, or ugly], but nevertheless it is an attempt to capture something not yet taken from life
into literature (that is, an experiment), and therefore
cannot be too harshly judged," the edge of criticism
is blunted. Nine tenths of the modern criticism of
modern experimental literature does in fact come down

to this; that the work, whatever it is, has obvious faults, but is original (that is, experimental), and therefore may be important. Even our criticism must be experimental until some at least of the experiments in art are concluded.

We are well rid, it is true, of the old dogmatisms where each authority huddled over his particular bone of theory and barked at every stranger. But we have a new dogmatism in an anti-puritanism which is in the worst sense puritanical. The radical experimenter, in literature or in life, will not tolerate fixed beliefs on the part of any one. He laughs at all certainty and condemns all principle. To be deductive, with him, is to be damned. The anti-puritan thinks it a heinous sin to refrain from satisfying any strong desire or principle, or to subdue your ego instead of expanding it, or to refrain from leaving a wife you no longer besottedly adore. The modern bohemia is a looking-glass land where all compulsions are reversed. In a dozen recent books one is made to feel that you must *not* be too moral, must *not* control your passions, must *not* sacrifice yourself for others, must *not* love your neighbor, or even your family, one quarter as much as yourself. And this is a corollary to a belief in unrestricted and all-important experiment.

Reaction has already set in against this belief that if we only look far enough through the world we are sure to find a way to settle everything; but I do not find it among these anti-puritans and the howlers down of the old régime. They are merely turning, turning upon the wheel of experiment, condemning, as they turn, all that lies behind them. No, the return to principle is to be found in less sententious books. I find it in Miss Zona Gale's and Miss Willa Cather's searchings for essential character as a durable thing, or among the English in Miss Sheila Kaye-Smith and the Galsworthy of "The Forsyte Saga." I find it in Edwin Arlington Robinson. I find it in the new literature of reverie, where the attempt, as in Sherwood Anderson, otherwise a notable experimenter, is to pierce beneath the drift of experience to the quality of that life itself which animates the individual man and, when set free, impels him. I find a sense of the necessity of coming to some conclusion as to what life is to mean for us in the criticism of Cabell and Santayana, the poetry of Masefield and Vachel Lindsay, and the lyrics of Miss Millay, which seem to spring, like the Jacobean and Carolingian poetry, from an inner and confident light. The center of gravity in all these books begins again to lie within and not without. The answer is sought in the mind and not in circumstance. There has been, so the authors seem to say, experience and expansion enough; now let us check the hurrying soul and question it for truth.

Yet it is not reaction, a mechanical movement at best, which we need so much as consummation, a harvesting of experiment. And here literature will inevitably wait upon life. It will run ahead of common belief, but after the minds that lead us. We shall have to resolve the problem of inside and outside before literature will cease to be endlessly eclectic. Perhaps that problem is insoluble except by faith. Perhaps we shall never prove whether there is dualism, as of spirit and body, or unity in life. It now seems unlikely that natural science will help us much further, for natural science has taken behavior as its sole reality and will not, or cannot, go behind the mechanics of that problem. Whether spiritualism or the new quasi-science of psychics will give light it is too soon to say. The credibility and the interpretation of the evidence submitted must first be tested. But some harmony between two conflicting and, so I believe, extreme tendencies—the reference of all our conduct and belief to the results of investigation, and a failure to consult nature at all in these matters—between, in short, behaviorism and tradition, can surely be attained. There is no soul-heal in science, no reason in the denial of ascertained fact. Neither Loeb nor Bryan can help us much in our philosophy. But we shall find again a *modus vivendi*.

And that mode of thinking about living must take into more account than has been popular in this age of free experiment the *integer vitæ*, the resolve to live finely rather than fully, the discipline which prevents excess, the generosity which implies self-sacrifice, the power to do without. All these qualities hamper experiment, but no experiment can unseat them as traits highly desirable in man. The self-restraint, the discipline, the godliness of one age, are not as those of another. John Milton grew too crabbed for use, and Addison too smug. Tennyson's code of morals seems out of perspective to-day, and Walt Whitman's song of the senses quite properly shames such priggishness. But neither a family nor a civilization can be raised on the principle of trying everything once. When shoe-strings are tight, we loosen them, and then, when the foot adjusts itself, tighten them a little again. So it is with over and under discipline. The old restraints are broken; it is time now to tighten belts.

And as soon as some clearer vision comes out of this murk of facts and factors in which historians, economists, novelists, biologists, poets, are twisting and turning, books will be respondent. It is probable that this age will then appear to have been pioneers' ground for the new order, in which we exploited the forest, broke up soil, tried our crops. Extraordinarily superficial much of our experimental literature will seem, of course. Perhaps the subtlest books, results of the most exhaustive experiments, will appear the most superficial, since it is there that men and women are analyzed into almost meaningless fact. Our literature will seem like a museum without a catalogue. "Why did he trouble to anatomize Main Street? Why did she describe the stream of consciousness in literal detail?" will be the questions, and the answer, "It was useful [or useless] experiment!"

There will be many to say here and now that the remedy for this St. Vitus's dance of experiment is a new theology, or refuge in the arms of Mother Church, or scientific positivism. That is not the necessary conclusion of the argument, which says no more than that it is time to look within for strength as well as without for solution by experiment. Even stoicism solved problems that biology and physics cannot touch. In any event, we may drop the silly snobbishness which has been contemptuous of the past. It was natural that readers and writers who were bent upon experiment should have been impatient with stabilized life and stabilized literature. There was little attraction in stories of people who tried to *hold in* for moderns who felt that their duty to the universe was to *push out*.

I quote from a recently published novel, whose title, characteristically, is "Self":

"She had denied herself nothing, she had united herself with a supreme passion to a perfect mate [a prize-fighter], but she had not changed. She had given him her body, only to find that her mind was still her own, richer and more finely colored by the experience through which she had passed." This faintly humorous transcript from the life of an adventuress is not really funny; it is merely logical. If you possessed a culture of rare germs, would you not try them in every environment you could think of, and watch them to see whether they grew or declined? That is how our novelists have felt about their characters, and will continue to feel until the urge to experiment gives place to the desire to conserve and refine. Naturally, the writer of such experimental books is largely indifferent to stable literature with ideals and a clear purpose, but that is no justification for a contemptuous underestimate. Thoreau and Emerson, to return to our own immediate past, formless as they were, with deficient technic and an undeniable pallor in the emotions of sex, yet tower over our immediate contemporaries with every indication of greatness. We are children of the inventive intellect of Franklin, who applied good sense to everything, and molded both his religion and his morals by what he could learn from his environment. He was a great and useful man; our writers, scholars, scientists, are useful also; if they seem to lack some element of greatness it is because their ends, though obtainable, concern no more than the health, conduct, prosperity, and emotional stimulation of man.

But Emerson and Thoreau were spiritual descendants of Jonathan Edwards and his kind. They were inhibited, as he was inhibited (inhibited, says a current play, is the modern word for being decent), in many directions. But their attempt (and this is a definition of their literary work) was to discipline and refine the emotions to deeper harmonies and finer perceptions. And this attempt has an absolute value entirely apart from the truth or untruth of transcendentalism, and different from the relative value of experiments which depends upon success. This study of perfection, very humanly conducted, gave to these men at their best a moral grandeur, which is a quality very highly to be appraised in literature, and one of the forms of beauty, which in its esthetic sense these writers did not always attain.

The New England of the forties and fifties was doubtless stifling to the free emotion and even to the eager intellect. It was too caste-bound and hidebound for much needed experiment. The adventurous in body went to sea or West. The mentally adventurous took to books, and found their cosmopolitanism in contact with the brains of the Old World and their expansion in contacts with nature. They were curiously content to live a village life, and unhappy when far away from their Concords. Having little society among the living, they were forced to raise themselves to the level of the great ones among the dead. The necessity produced innumerable freaks and vagarists, moonshiny minds like Alcott's, founders of quaint religions, mystics who lost their sense of reality. It also brought forth rare eminence of mind and fineness of spirit. But our cosmopolitanism of world-wide experiment is too easy. Any one can rise to the level of Broadway, and, if they are shrewd, observe there. We are all sensible, all worldly, all tolerant, all conversant with reality. How to gird up one's loins and climb has almost been forgotten.

The plain people of the same forties and fifties, when they spoke of a good book, meant a righteous book. We think that their conception of literature was pitifully narrow, and are surely right. But a good book, to deserve the title, should at least have sustenance in it. These endless experiments with impressions, moods, glands, psychoses, complexes, repressions, are beginning to lose their interest. These interminable biographies of adolescence, and what love did to it and what it did to love, grow tedious. In a recent contest for a prize novel hundreds of manuscripts followed this pattern, and, like the saints' legends of the Middle Ages, were so much alike in style and plot that they could be more readily classified by localities than by the names of their authors. Yes, we are cosmopolitan, we are acquainted with the peculiarities of life in every climate and under all conditions of sub- and supernormality; we know how to explain our social habits and our personal traits: but as to what is to be done with them and about them when all is investigated, we seem lamentably incurious.

Expansion and contraction in cycles is a characteristic of literature as well as of business. There is one kind of literary contraction now pinching us which I do not mean to praise in this essay—the contraction of fear. The prohibitionists and the timorously minded who fear for their conventions are attacking the freer emotional life which experiment has certainly given us. The censors desire to paralyze the literary nerve. They wish it to vibrate only by permission. For experiment which may wander into the forbidden regions of sex, they would substitute a canalized stream of limited consciousness.

The contraction, I predict, has nothing to do with such debased puritanism as this. It will bring with it a subtle change in emphasis. Man will begin to mean more; his adventures, less. Morality will begin to mean more than morale, and may get a new definition. The ego, having passed through the laboratory and been dressed and undressed in every street, will once more become an instrument by which we strive to attain an ideal, although that ideal may differ widely from the ideals popular in books on the will-to-power, in boy-scout meetings, and the college Y. M. C. A. We shall look more to Confucius and less to Casanova. Thus the heart will be shaped, and afterward new books will be shaped also. Experiment has years to run yet, and I, as a man of my time, still follow its literary revelations with fascinated interest. I should regard an age of no experiment as a racial catastrophe. And yet, like the financier, excited and yet troubled by a business boom expanding and expanding beyond the needs of society, I look for an antidote to excess, and, in literature expect to find it in thoughts bent inward.

The Expressionists

MR. EDMUND WILSON, JR., in an illuminating essay, has explained what those modernists in the arts, the so-called expressionists, are trying to achieve. He finds in the Western World an esthetic solidarity among many who feel the wild tide of the times rising in their hearts. And he asserts that with these moderns the impulse to express is stronger than the power or desire to interpret; that the world as they see it cannot be interpreted because it is chaotic, incoherent, meaningless. They reflect its indigestion of unorganized elements and believe that to do this vividly is art. As the leader of the dadaists has elsewhere said (I paraphrase his jargon in plain American), it is a foolish world, therefore let us be foolish too in representing it.

Mr. Wilson makes his criticism, which we who still cling desperately to sanity will not dispute, that even if the world is nothing, we in self-respect must try to make something out of it. In every age, he says, men have placed their own arbitrary interpretation upon the mysteries of evolution and devolution, and we also must assume a theory of life and, if we choose to write of the world, make sense and not nonsense. For whatever life may be, art must be coherent.

This is a sound criticism, but as a defense of ordered

of interpretation as with a self-willed desire to use new knowledge to justify us in emptying out a hodge-podge of emotions, and in making the hitherto inexpressible the only theme.

I write in general terms because it is, after all, not the writers so much as the critics that I am attacking. Traces of this expressionism run mad can be found in all the Americans whom we call new and modern—in Anderson, in Cabell, in Waldo Frank, in Dreiser. In many freakish experiments, and in such a notable book as "Ulysses" or such a striking poem as "The Waste Land" it may be seen full-fledged. But it is not the books so much as the tendency, and particularly the critical defense of the tendency, which must be fought. The books share and reflect, sometimes with exaggeration, the moral confusion of our world; the critics erect a philosophy of incoherence and cheer their victims on towards anarchy.

Let us drop therefore specific books, and drop especially the expressionism of sex, which is only a part of the question, as it is only a part of ordered life. What we see among writers who are over sensitive to the time spirit is a desperate dropping of all standards and certainties, and a scurry through experience to see what is left. This is not true of modern literature as a whole, but it is characteristic of that marginal fringe which marks our advance toward progress or decay.

For example, in scores of poems, plays, novels, fantasies, written by the advanced few for the few, the heroes are personalities shedding husk after husk of accepted belief and expected conduct, with no stopping place, no kernel in sight. I find this true of Mr. Lawrence's figures and of the central characters of the new American realists. It is true of less experimental literature. Babbitt is such a figure, as would have been manifest if Mr. Lewis had been writing fiction instead of satire.

Well, if this is reality, why should we object? If the sensitive modern mind finds existence a chaos, history a falsification, religion a sham, science an illusion, morality a code, and personality a series of complexes, why naturally the owner of that mind will be affected. His thoughts can have no unity; his emotions can lead nowhere; he will be adrift upon the stream of consciousness. And this is true of more men and women, especially young men and women, than we care to admit. They are disintegrating, and society, like an old wall, shows the cracks and the crumbles where they have slipped out like mortar that will hold no longer.

The value of the novelists, the poets, and the dramatists in this new school of expressionism is precisely that they are telling us this. They are demanding freedom to express everything because there is, they think, no other way to describe a revolution whose end is anarchy, physical, moral, and intellectual. They are screaming protests against the fatheads who believe that society can run on conventional religion, conventional morality, conventional thinking indefinitely. They belong, indeed, to those spiritual pioneers who in every generation push on ahead into a future not yet realized, often never realized. These suffer vicariously for the rest of us, are tortured by the implications of our philosophy, frightened by the dangers of our conduct, appalled by the application of our knowledge. It may be reformation they demand, or it may be expressionism; they may be right, or they may be wrong; but they are always important because they register the temperature of humanity and its blood pressure. By them we may diagnose both health and disease, and this is the answer to those who complain of the attention given to seeming freakishness.

The seers of this generation have undoubtedly looked upon chaos. The War has sharpened their vision, but there is more behind them than the War. For a century we have been breeding eclecticism, inconsistency, conflict of knowledge and belief. The stronger minds have thrown over tradition, not in contempt, but in distrust and unwillingness to lean upon uncertainty. And these same strong minds have found no alternative but a vague mysticism, or a crude materialism, which as a philosophy science is already attacking by disproving the substantiability of matter, its base. Faith, philosophy, conduct, purposes seem all alike chaotic; only scientific research in its narrow area, and mechanical development of the products of the earth's crust are firm, coherent, sure in results. But their results, so great upon the visible world, are petty otherwise. All this the plain man escapes by taking refuge in a tolerable present. All this the weakly sensitive see, and rush to the foolish generalization that the world is chaos, personality incoherent, themselves mere clusters of unrelated experience. And the writer who makes us understand that this is happening is valuable—be he cubist, dadaist, expressionist, or Freudo-fictionist; but his art is not therefore great. If he has no detachment, no perspective himself, his art is probably bad, no matter how informative.

For art, which must interpret, must therefore be coherent, whatever may be the superficial appearance of life. It is true that the coherence of life is only a hypothesis, but it is a hypothesis concomitant with the existence of man as a rational and self-respecting being, and art, if it is to be human, must support the theory. Furthermore, the art of literature does not deal primarily with the stream of consciousness which for us humans is life; it deals with man's attitudes towards life, with the love of beauty, with self-sacrifice, with honor, with self-control, with religion. There is nothing incoherent here, no lack of absolutes, although definitions may vary. These attitudes, indeed, are not perhaps definable; they are not straight lines, or points, they are areas in which each man must define his own absolutes. That he does so, that men and women, whom we all admire, whom even the expressionists admire, have done so in every generation, is not open to doubt. The readiness—to make life coher-

ent, to live coherently, to write coherently—is all, as
Hamlet said in another connection, but so saying meant
what I mean.

If this is true, or even relatively true, then we must
praise the expressionist as a safety valve while remaining most doubtful as to the permanent value of
the steam he emits. We must say, what even the expressionist knows in his cooler moments and exhibits
in his better work, that restraint is justified even when
the world seems most incoherent. The stoic was no
fool. Neither is he who would exercise self-control,
the virtue of the Puritan, without his vices. To stand
squarely in an age of thoughtless haste and morbid in-
conclusion is better than to slide with a clutter of all
our dishes down the backstairs of civilization, which
seems to be the ambition of some of our most literate.
These experimenters are brilliant; they will give us a
new technique before they are done; they have already
given new subjects to art, and new, and some of them
true, views of life. But we need not believe that they
are prophets of an age of anarchy and negation. Of
course, that is possible, and if you must believe it, you
will. But it is more probable that they are only ex-
plorers, lost and crashing through the jungle between
the old trail and a better one.

I will be as pessimistic as the most pessimistic intellectual where material progress and its future are
concerned, but not as to the eternal value of self-
control, clear thinking, and with these delight and

beauty eagerly sought. It is an attitude which can be translated into terms of criticism, and then it means that we have better grounds than mere timorous necessity for resisting the chaotic, the incoherent, and the unrestrained in literature and in all art.

Going Deeper

TWENTY years ago critics used to write of Realism with a big R, as if there were some one Real Thing in life which ought to be put into literature. We hear less of realism now, and the cause is that we begin to understand how relative is the appearance of reality. Man in the twelfth century was very like man in the twentieth, but the reality he presented to an Abélard, who believed that flesh was grass, was very different from the reality Mr. Wells sees in him. In fact, every change in our philosophy of life, whether springing from a shift in religion or a discovery in science, affects our conception of reality and is reflected in the mirror of life, which is literature. When the nineteenth century demonstrated evolution our conception of What Man Is began sensibly to alter, and literature quickly responded. The erection of psychology into a science was followed by the psychological novel. The recent discoveries in the subconscious have hard upon their heels a literature of reverie and subconscious impulse.

Professor Cross feels that novels, in which the author goes groping through the psychologies of his characters looking for motives, impulses, and neuroses, are unsatisfactory by comparison with earlier fiction. Where Smollett, Thackeray, Dickens studied people, these new novelists study theories of what men and women subjectively must be like. They approach reality only by projecting outward their own inner experiences. Thackeray could test his Colonel Newcome by the acts of real colonels, but Sherwood Anderson can try the hidden impulses of his characters solely by the experience of the only inner man he really knows.

We must accept the criticism. The novel, play, or poem that dabbles in the subconsciousness now is usually either experimental, like May Sinclair's later novels, where you seem to see a proposition in italics at the head of each chapter, or highly personal, as in Anderson's stories, where one queries, Is this subconscious man or just recently conscious Anderson? But that the novel of the subconsciousness is to be a failure because it can never be truly written I do not believe. It is hard to guess at the inner life of another, but not so much more difficult than to grasp the very picture and significance of his outer life. Intuition is required for each, and into the most objective of characters some of the author's own personality enters. If, instead of drawing Tom Jones or Mr. Pickwick, it is the submerged personality of a neurotic woman that interests the writer, the difference in faculties required is probably only an intuition attuned to more subtle intimacies of thought and emotion. The thing can certainly be done, and it is certainly neither more nor less worth doing. It is not a new feat, but only a new development in creation.

And it will be done because we shall increasingly wish to know more and more of the inner life of men and women. With the standardizations of life and the equalization of the classes superficial distinctions are being planed away. The world is being Americanized. Plumbers and professors begin *apparently* to resemble each other in everything but taste and special knowledge. The clergyman and the realtor are interchangeable in conversation and appearance. Women, in emancipating themselves, have become *apparently* like men. There was more evident variety in dress, personality, opinion, and manner in an English railway compartment of, say, 1850 than in a train of Pullmans to-day.

And as our exteriors grow more and more alike the novelist is bound to go deeper and deeper in search of the vital distinctions that make the constant drama of life. He knows that under the indifferent bustle of a modern city, where nothing seems to happen that is not trivial, intense emotions are playing, not less, but more violent because convention restrains them. Perforce he must and will dip into the subconscious if the trail leads there. Science has given him what his predecessors lacked—a faith in his own intuitions. Experimental at first, his way of looking at life in ten years will be as familiar as the Elizabethan drama. We may hope in so rich a field for great books.

Outlook and Insight

Does Mr. Hergesheimer look at the world about him before he begins to write, or at his own soul? Are Miss Lowell and Mr. Galsworthy and Mr. Masters and Mr. Tarkington outlookers or inseers? The question is more fundamental than it sounds.

For years, until this simple test had been applied, we supposed ourselves afloat in a great subjective period. Never was such a time for the psychology of inbroodings and the analyses of suppressed and un-suppressed emotions. Never (it seemed) were there so many novelists who professed a philosophy half-baked or hard-boiled sometimes, but still a philosophy. Never did poets so ardently seek to catch the subtle subjective mood by a poignant image, fascinatingly obscure. Never were there so many books published on the inner working of man's machine. And yet never did a voluminous literature so passionately and meticulously register the world about it. Never were special cases, such as diseased souls and harsh environments, indeed every fact which is subject to observation, so popular. Never at one time were so many sharp-sighted observers telling us what life was like, or ought to be like, or would be like day after to-morrow.

Is this a paradox? Not at all. It is the age of outlook, not insight. Insight is a fruit of meditation, not of theorizing or of observing. It springs from familiarity with one's own soul, which (whatever definition you give to soul) is a very different thing from familiarity with one's own psychological reactions. How many writers to-day seem really familiar with their own souls? Are there ten among those excellent in English?

No, the outlookers have it all their own way just now in English and a very good way they are making of it. Materials for the psychological history of the period are mounting hill high, and many of the books that contain them are honest and skilful art that will endure. But is it querulous to ask for more inseers, men like St. Paul who write from a passionate meditation, or quiet people who compose not so much to describe as to express? Universal education seems to be making students of all of us, whose first duty is to study the visible world and report.

Mr. Robinson among Americans seems to be an inseer and so does Mr. Frost, although a careless reader might think differently. No American novelist since Hawthorne, except, perhaps, Melville, has belonged wholly in that category, although we suspect Miss Cather may force us to make that statement less absolute. Abroad there is James Stephens in Ireland in his own quaint way, and there is Walter de la Mare. "The Memoirs of a Midget" was a puzzling book. Critics praised without describing it, readers admired without altogether comprehending it. And yet here was surely an example of inseeing sprung among all our outlooking like a pink lady's-slipper in a forest of familiar growth. This writer looked at his own sensitive poet's soul, saw it was different, whimsically different from other souls, despaired of explaining it, did not care to adventure out into the world describing, like the others, what he saw there of other people's souls and their adventures. So home he came and invented a tiny creature whose physical ratio to ordinary humanity was in delicacy just as the poet's soul to our prosaic one. And then he told what the midget felt in life. That is a typical product of inseeing before outlooking, and this is why the book seemed so original, is original, and, for our day, unique.

The airs that blow through the present are clearly not favorable for such a manner of living, thinking, writing. Or is it that we merely think them unfavorable, and run madly here and there studying the habits of the species like the rest? Well, the literary plants we grow are brave, bright-colored fellows, fluttering with vivid details and hung with fat fruits of philosophy. Yet now and then one longs for some less sappy, stalky vegetables, for something with *roots*, deep roots that go down and down into the deep earth of long meditation.

Cervantes said, paraphrasing earlier inseers, "Make it thy business to know thyself, which is the most difficult lesson in the world." We wonderfully know our neighbors—but ourselves? Let him who is certain of the answer cast the first vote!

Longfellow Junior

THE United States is the happy home and fertile breeding ground of the magazine. We invented the literary, illustrated magazine, of which the old *Harper's* was a prototype; we invented *The Saturday Evening Post;* we invented *The Literary Digest;* we invented (and will some day ask to be forgiven) that neat combination of pictures, gossip, good advice, and stories of getting rich easily that just now dominates the news-stands. We did not invent the magazine of experiment, but we have most expensively fostered it.

Conservative readers have not been fair to these magazines of experiment. A cover like a grenade exploding in a worm fence, or a page of familiar words arranged like poetry, but meaning nothing, or a story full of unmentionables, has put them off before they have begun to read. But an experimental magazine must, after all, experiment or lack justification, and among these experiments some, in a well-conducted journal, are likely to prove highly successful, while there is room between the adventures in literature for good things that any one can read. So it has been with these magazines. To all, but to *The Dial* particularly, which now has history behind it, we owe a debt, that will later be acknowledged, for printing what more timorous journals feared to print and for making accessible to American readers the forward fringe of literary experiment abroad. We are supposed to be naïvely old fashioned in our literary tastes; yet what other country makes such a determined effort to keep abreast of the world's latest in esthetic emotion?

We could devote the remainder of this essay to praise of the enterprise and the audacity of the editors of these journals and the Europe in English which they have given us. Indeed—and the compliment may startle them—they are the Longfellows and the Bayard Taylors of this American period. As Longfellow brought back Germany and Scandinavia in his carpet bag and Tennyson in his hip pocket, so have these modern civilizers brought the very latest in Munich, Moscow, and Milan over to us. They hate Longfellow and all his works, but their service and his are identical.

Unfortunately, their conception of American literature seems also to resemble Longfellow's. Not content with making our grandfathers *au courant* with the latest in Continental poetry, he founded a school of his own in Cambridge where American themes could be treated in the best European fashion. He gave us "Hiawatha" and "Evangeline," much better poems than the Longfellow juniors of the new magazines are willing to admit, but still imitative and not really American. *The Dial* apparently would have us make the same mistake over again. Here, its editors say— by implication and sometimes directly—here is the way to write; these are the subjects, these the methods of modern European literature; go you and do likewise and we shall have an American literature! A hyphenated literature we may thus get perhaps, a new school of Russo-Germano-Yiddo-Anglo-American literature, in historical position like that which Longfellow conducted in Cambridge three-quarters of a century ago, but in character and quality very different, and probably inferior. Longfellow, when all is said against him, remains a remarkably versatile talent; Lowell would not readily find his intellectual equal in New York to-day; Holmes was no dabster either!

But we do not want another age of Longfellow. Bring Europe to us by all means and in every measure. Encourage us to experiment, break down the prejudices that withhold us from novelty, fertilize the American soil with ideas from abroad; but don't tell us to write like Schnitzler, D. H. Lawrence, or Paul Fort, or any one else whose environment and tradition are utterly different from our own. Ever since the mid-eighteenth century, when Americans began to feel that they were not Europeans, some worthy missionary or another has been bringing in Europe to civilize us, saying: "Drink this; then act like little Europeans, and your souls will be saved." And those who like Hawthorne refused to act, or who, like Walt Whitman and Mark Twain, rejected the cup, have best pleased both the Europeans and ourselves. We thank *The Dial* and the rest for giving us more of Europe, but will not join them in acting Longfellow over again. That play is out of date.

Gin and Nonsense

NOBODY objects to nonsense except Puritans, who used to dislike it because frivolity was shocking in God's temple, which was man, and efficiency experts, who distrust it because it wastes time that might be used in getting things done. For the rest of us, a little life not too strictly chaperoned by sense is as valuable as tobacco or yawning. Flippancy, flirting, spoofing, giggling, repartee, and the milder varieties of naughtiness are part of every day. And so, of course, they get into books. "Alice in Wonderland," "The Bab Ballads," "The Mikado," "The Autocrat of the Breakfast Table" drew off, among other things, the nonsense of that nineteenth century society which on carpets under gas lamps was so content with its world that it could jest without bitterness.

Nonsense has more edge in our time. There is more satire in it than fooling; the best-natured columnists keep hatpins in their typewriters, and their nonsense, like everything else nowadays, is more self-conscious than it used to be. It has become, indeed, a profession, and in comic strips and movies a kind of peasant art which some day will be collected and edited.

But there is another kind of humor much less good-natured than fooling and seldom appearing in contented societies. The angry satirists—Ben Jonson,

Butler, Swift, and Pope, the cynical satirists, Congreve and Byron and Oscar Wilde—these men put alcohol in their nonsense. They wrote to amuse by exposing. Their work is a libel on society, and if you believed all they said you would go out to the stable, like Gulliver, and live with the horses. They are scurrilous against men who are worse than they ought to be and insinuating toward women who are lighter than they ought to be, and usually they are either indecent or blasphemous or suggestive.

And we have always agreed that such defamers of society, who tell the truth about its backstair doings, should have a very special skill if they were to be regarded as more than scandalmongers. It is true that if you desire easy notoriety the readiest way is to print the unprintable, but that is not the way to make books live. Whole shopfuls of indiscreet or violent books have gone down into oblivion, while those that have lived, like "The Way of the World," the epigrams of Martial, "Candide," "The Rape of the Lock," and "Lady Windermere's Fan," have survived because of some quite transcending grace or power or penetration which has made their satire permanent.

Satirists of our loose-living prosperity should take heed. There is too much gin and nonsense in fiction and drama and too little power and art. "A wild time was had by all" is thought to be enough to make a chapter or an act or a short story. The social satirist of to-day spares no expense in fictitious cocktails, but afterwards is content to describe what his characters say and do in their illegal exaltation. He doubles the number of kisses and thinks that he has increased the intensity of his book.

In this country the unsteady experiments of Scott Fitzgerald have been responsible for many imitations that lack his flashes of genius. There is a gin school of literature in which the society depicted is synthetic, like its liquor. No charm of personality, no revelation of human nature, no wit, no fine scorn justifies such books. They have no merit except as moving pictures of flashy living. To a libertine of 1700 they would seem naïve and to a belated Victorian they must seem trivial as social documents and misguided as art. Prohibition has favored the increase of this new variety of "shocker" by making naughtiness out of what before 1919 was not worth writing about. Indeed, there is a real danger that for some time young ladies who play rough and tumble and young men who carry flasks will be regarded as romantic figures defying convention, and therefore, however vapid, material for literature. Those who remember what dull trash are the stories of romantic heroes imitated from Byron who defied the world as a relief for their swollen egoes, will guess what will become of the gin and nonsense literature of to-day. Neither one cocktail nor many, one love affair nor many, are in themselves enough to make an enduring book.

The Shortage in Fiction

THE trouble with American fiction is that there is not enough of it. How can the hundred thousand good readers, which we may fairly assume in the United States, be satisfied by five or ten novels and perhaps thirty short stories a year? For that is about the sum total of good American fiction.

There is plenty of sociology. Dull books, describing typical conditions, full of typical people, who lead typical lives, books composed in honest labor, with a painful exactitude of description, and not one spark of personal emotion, not one lift of imagination in a hundred pages—of these there are dozens, and they are much praised by intellectuals, and their authors patted dutifully for their "unsparing realism" and a "true picture" of America.

There is plenty of propaganda. Books with burning theses, books with stupid theses, books with crazy theses, are given feature advertising and are talked of as if they were fiction. They are read, too, in thousands by those who wish to improve themselves by reading "thoughtful books." Doubtless when there is some truth in the lesson such books do good, take the place perhaps of the weekly sermon, but they are not novels.

There is a cascading torrent of commercialized sentimentalism. The so-called writer of American fiction is nine times in ten not a creator at all, but a shrewd individual possessed of a vocabulary who has learned to feed the illusions of the multitudes. He looks not into his own heart, but into theirs, and with a skilful technique tells better than we can the crude stories of success in love or riches, of heroic self-sacrifice and escape which we all cherish, and spin to ourselves between sleeping and waking. He exploits our rather weak imaginings, instead of creating new meat for us to feed upon. He is a parasite; his work is second hand and second rate, with a machine-made accuracy and no deep emotion whatsoever. Like the makers of the ancient ballads, these modern writers for the community give up their individuality when they compose. They sell their names for cash and henceforth are indistinguishable by anything else.

There are more neurotic books than the supply of neurotics justifies. Paucity of ideas, lack of invention, need not prevent you from writing if your brain is unhealthily excited by morbid experience. With the solemnity which belongs to the especially enlightened, you may become a specialist in the shady side of the soul, or an expert in the grossities of the body, and achieve a pathologist's reputation without the fatigue of study. Such books are always informing, although sometimes they tell more of the author than of his characters; sometimes they are brilliant, especially when they run a temperature; but they are not real novels.

And what is a real novel? Not, be sure, a book that requires a complex rhetorical definition, but merely a lengthy story with human characters, written by a novelist who is an artist, out of the depths of his own experience. A painter must be able to draw; a musician must have an ear. We have been too much afflicted with dozens of so-called novelists who lack absolutely the sense of the beautiful, the feeling for form, the creative power of imagination which a writer who is an artist must have. Plot-builders, sensation-mongers, ultra-realists, psychologists, specialists in business, war, sex, New Thought, the desert, the heroic West, the younger generation—they may have the equipment for successful production; but what of that if they cannot write? They serve their very useful purposes when they serve any one but themselves, but they are not real novelists if they cannot write.

And no book is a real book, least of all a novel a real novel, without a real man or a real woman behind it. The conception of the ineffectual, ill-balanced genius capturing the truth of the world through his own weakness is a fiction. Holding the mirror up to nature is a misleading phrase. It is not nature but nature in oneself that must be reflected, and if the self is colorless so will be the picture. Egoistic novels are the expression of selves that are expressive, but inexperienced. Not that way lies our need, but rather for personalities which can carry the vibrations of their world. Real novels are not anemic or superficial, like so much in American fiction. One can feel the pulse of life beating in them and know that the blood comes richly from a great heart.

II

America in Literature

Americans in Fiction

THE subject indicated by the title above is extensive enough for an encyclopedia, ambitious enough for a book. Let me hasten to explain, therefore, that in this essay I purpose no more than some suggestions of literary assets we have not yet utilized. The writer, as well as the critic, may profitably delve more deeply.

There is already much more in literature of the social and esthetic history of Americans than hasty generalizers realize. Our critics have discussed American literature in terms of greatness. The question has been, Who can be put beside Carlyle or Maupassant, Dickens or Matthew Arnold, as a literary figure of great magnitude? But the historian sees things differently. He looks for the imagination of a race and the facts of their behavior, and sometimes a second-rate book will tell him more than a masterpiece. He will get most from the masterpieces, but lesser works concern him also. American literature has never been thoroughly studied for the history of the American mind and for light on the American character. It will prove to be rich.

It will prove to be rich; and in the meantime the question, What sort of information do American books yield most readily about America and the Americans? inspires new questions, and suggests some interesting reflections upon the lacks and possessions of our national literature.

One conclusion which any shelf of American fiction chronologically arranged will drive home is that if we did not invent local color, we have carried it as far as any modern nation. Here was a country geographically very much the same through vast areas, and a population which despite its diverse sources had to face very much the same difficulties of life and livelihood in the North, South, East, and West. As the old charter for the settlement of the "Western Lands" of Connecticut on the Housatonic had it, a settler must "subdue and fence" six acres before he could get valid title to his tract. Americans at the beginning were all subduers of land, and many have remained so until this day. Nevertheless, in many of our most famous books, and in all the histories of literature, there appears from a very early period a notable sectionalism which has made it fatally easy to classify American authors. The first thing to do, of course, with an author is to classify him for ready reference; many seem to think that it is also the last. We had our New England school, our stories of the Southern cavaliers, our Indiana group, our pioneer narratives, and we are now in the midst of an attack of the Wild West.

This sectional literature is useful to the historian when it is not too much sentimentalized, and it has given us some great books; but it is no longer promising. The Wild West film of the movies and the novel of "the great open spaces" in brilliant slip cover are examples of literature gone to seed. There is little truth and no health, but only crude excitement and fabricated sentiment. in most of them. The sectional stories were great only when they struck beneath environment into something of the mind which was valuable entirely apart from the influences that helped a little to mold it. Hawthorne did this for New England, Melville and Cooper for the American sea, Mark Twain for the Mississippi Valley. Willa Cather for the plains, Sinclair Lewis for the Western town or city, are doing it to-day.

In the South, so it seems to me, local color went to seed before it was ripe. It was richer and more glamorous there, but it remained just local color. The great poet of the South, Poe, was inspired by sectionalism not at all; his second, Lanier, was scarcely more Southern than he; the novelists and short-story writers who have given us a dozen Souths, all equally picturesque, have stayed upon the level of manners. The great Southern story is yet to be written, and it will have to be more than a Southern story to succeed.

The rather thin cream of local color (a better figure than seed-time) has been skimmed, and racial fiction promises no better returns. It is our habit to say, "Look at the immigrants, the wonderful richness of their native minds and spirits, the dramatic contrasts between them and new environment!" A born writer cannot see a booted Russian peasant woman in a subway car without desiring to write a story about her.

And yet there has been very little really important written about our immigrants. Their differences from us are picturesque; but in themselves they touch us and become part of us through their resemblances, and after the first generation the resemblances outweigh the differences ten to one. It may be true that the second and third generation Italians will have something new to contribute to American life, but as material for fiction they are most interesting as would-be Americans struggling to become standardized. Their strain too closely resembles our own to hold its difference long. I doubt if any one ever writes a great novel, for example, where the major interest is the Germanness of a German emigrant or the essential Russianism of the Russian Americans. The alien will provide a background, a sub-plot for fiction, which is as yet only glanced at in our literature. But as a subject for American literature our immigrants of the present flow are likely to be just picturesque in the first generation, commonplace in the second, the period of adaptation, and in the third best written of as American.

The exception among racial aliens, of course, is the negro, whose literature is just beginning. Special circumstances make him more at home in America than the rest, and yet keep him further apart. He has appeared in our literature as propaganda, as folk-lore, as comic relief, and as sentiment. His nature is rich, his situation always somewhat tragic, his experience unexampled in the history of barbarians quickly civ-

ilized. The appearance of Stribling's "Birthright" and
Shands's "White and Black" was a herald of a new
literature of the negro. As material for American literature he is the least worked, but not the easiest.
Probably the literature of the American negro can
be written only by himself.

The American regarded as a creation of his own history is also getting to be thin pickings for literature.
At present the pioneer is receiving his romantic recognition, just as the Virginia cavalier got his in the
nineties. It was only a little while ago that we realized
suddenly that generation after generation cannot push
their pioneering activities on and on to the Pacific
without creating a pioneer's psychology for the nation.
History elaborated this idea, and fiction and poetry,
spelling the pioneer with a P, has clast a glamour upon
the hewer of trees and wielder of the plow.

But already we grow a little weary of the heroic in
this mold, and are more interested in the individuality
of the descendant than in the pioneering qualities he
may have inherited.

The solemn truth is that the pioneer as such was a
better figure for epic than for familiar fiction. The
frontier was a rather distressing place at all times, a
border of flotsam and jetsam, whisky-runners and
half-breeds, rough-necks seeking freedom to be tough
quite as abundantly as vigorous spirits in search of
mental elbow-room and a competence. The best pioneers are still Cooper's, who, if he idealized Deerslayer,
gave us the Ishmael Bush family in somber, sordid

power. Too many pioneering families over which romance kindles in actuality may have resembled the mountaineer, his thousand hogs, and his giant daughter, whom Clarence King describes so vividly in the California of the sixties. The historical novel has still a great task to perform for our frontier days, and the poet may follow; but no American novelist can now be sure of inspiration just by saying, "I shall write of America as a land of pioneers."

Sectionalism and the frontier gave us country and town. More recently the city, the highly standardized and somewhat cosmopolitan city of our modern experience, has entered American literature. We have used our city life in two senses, for satire, as Sinclair Lewis, directly in "Babbitt," indirectly in "Main Street," has used it, and for the anti-romance of grim and sordid stories of the dullness of brick walls and cramped hearts. Writers have come to the cities to study commonplace people, neither pioneers nor Puritans nor Cavaliers, but people with vices and pimpled faces and uncertain ends. When the literary sum for this decade is totted, it will be seen that despite the exploitation everywhere of the West as the chief popular interest in fiction, the city, the city large enough to be like New York, and yet not too large to keep a unified character, has been the dominant note of really worthy fiction. More is to come of this. I doubt whether the fiction and drama of the city have even yet reached maturity. It has more of a future than the literature of regions, of races, and of the pioneer.

Nevertheless, I miss something even here, and certainly in the rest of this panorama of a national literature thus briefly outlined. I miss what I get in the Wessex tales of Hardy. I miss what I find in "The Brothers Karamazov" of Dostoevski. I miss specifically what the best of the Elizabethans and the strongest Victorians gave England. And here I am not speaking of high art, of style, of mere magnitude of conception, but rather of a quality which is definitive, not comparative, a method of studying humanity rather than an excellence or defect in the rendering thereof.

Put it this way. There seem to be three stages, rough and irregular, to be sure, but still observable stages, in national literatures. First comes among colonies and offshoots of established nations the imitative stage, where men write in terms of an older and stronger literature. This was illustrated once in English-speaking history when the Anglo-Saxons began to sophisticate their own language, with Latin as their model. It was illustrated equally well by our own earliest national literature. Colonial literature in America was simply British literature crudely written, or if it was powerful, like Jonathan Edwards's books, there was no nationalism in it except his own, which was as British as Hume's or Berkeley's. But the American writing of Irving's period began to be consciously American; yet the terms were British, the style, the characterization, the thought only relatively American.

Next follows, in many instances and certainly in the United States, a period intensely nationalistic where the writers are supersensitive to race or locality or national characteristics. Their books are, from one point of view, special documents explaining a new variety of the *genus homo*. This, of course, may happen more than once in the history of a nation. With us it is a characteristic of the prose fiction of before the Civil War; of the local-color stories of the last third of the century, and again of the nineties. Hawthorne, to choose a great name, was almost morbidly aware of New England and the New-Englanders; the short stories of Craddock, Cable, Hopkinson Smith, Margaret Deland, and all those genre writers who filled the best magazines in the days before 1900, were little tours about America in search of the native in its more intense and "original" aspects. In the nineties Richard Harding Davis and his followers and contemporaries in the new romantic school, successfully illustrated by Gibson, gave us the American as he liked to see himself after the Spanish War, clean, handsome, and cool. Nationalism had run a full arc from the psychological, through the picturesque, to romance.

But it had not run full circle. There is a further stage of nationalism in literature, where we accept our nationality, are indeed imbued with it, and yet write of a man as a man.

At this stage we grow weary of the American who

is put into fiction to illustrate something which the writer thinks is the truth about America; and that, I believe, is where we are at the present moment. There is valuable satiric writing yet to be done in what might be called the second phase of nationalism, as Mr. Lewis's brilliant and searching "Babbit," already mentioned, proves. But, satire aside, the great literary conquests are to be made not in nationalism, but in a humanity which is only secondarily American. Such future figures of fiction will be American in the nationalistic sense if you please, but that will not be the main point. Their creators will take nationality as a matter of course, or rather as something as definitely established as the rocks or the soil. Self-conscious Americanism will give way to the study of man in America.

I look for more strong writers who will seize upon folks as they are, and not as symbols of a developing civilization. The pioneer, the captain of industry, the grafting politician, the reformer—we know them pretty well as American types because novels about typical Americans have resembled a moving-picture labeled "Americans"; yet these figures, whether created by Dreiser or Howells or Norris, remain a little shadowy as men. There is always a touch of propaganda, often of caricature, to them.

I will not say that the fiction and the poetical narrative of the last few years is better than earlier American writing. We have yet to equal Hawthorne and the utterly un-nationalistic Poe. Yet certainly we are beginning to work away from self-consciousness. I like the hero of Miss Cather's "One of Ours," Claude, who could find nothing to arouse him in Kansas, and was happy in the War. He is utterly American, inconceivable as a member of any other nation, and yet there is nothing in the novel except its title, "One of Ours," to make that seem to be the reason for the book. He is Claude because he is American, but he is in a novel because he is Claude. And the greatest novel of the last decade, "Spoon River Anthology," which is no worse fiction for being written in verse, and no less a novel in effect because its plot comes together not in the book, but in the imagination of the reader—that was a remarkable study of the absolutely American, and as innocent of self-conscious nationalism as "The Return of the Native." But I am more interested in pointing the road than in making a bibliography.

And it is high time that the novelists are leaving description of our manners and finding us out. Under the deceptive standardization to which everything in America, except our sufferings and our fate, is being submitted, vibrates the greatest emotional energy of the modern world. I do not say the deepest or the finest or the best-directed emotion. The satirists are probably right in denying it these qualities. A vast amount of our energy, as Mr. Briggs reminds us daily, if we see what he means, is exhausted upon trivial ills and more trivial ambitions. It wreaks itself upon the conventionalized experience of getting business done, of establishing a standard home, and of living and loving as much like our neighbors as possible. Yet that in the mass it is a vibrating energy of intense power, no one who has the opportunity to compare American experience with western European can doubt. Its surplus spills over into riotous forms of excess, in the press, in athletics, in organization for the sake of organizing, in astonishing religious sects, and in ebullient philosophies of incredible optimism. The temptation to describe such a civilization by its normal, which is to say, its most evident and therefore most superficial, products is very great. There has never been a mass civilization like it, and thus mass description, where, as I have said, the hero is first of all a character picture of the current American, seems to be the most promising job for the writer of fiction. Not so. That is why we get folks who typify, rather than folks who are folks. That is why the more intellectual novelists lean to satire, because satire has always been the easiest way to throw light upon tendencies, characteristics, failings which are nation wide. When the stream of human nature is canalized, and for a moment seems to flow all one way, satire springs from the creative brain. But something more penetrating than a mass portrait, more sympathetic than satire, is needed to get what is happening to personality in this our America.

There was a real danger in the nineties that we readers would accept the romantic view of the iron-chinned, clear-eyed American as representing ourselves. Perhaps two-thirds of the movie audiences still do so, but the remainder, and those who do not live by the movies, are much too sophisticated for that. It is significant that instead of idealizing the young American, as we did after the Spanish War, to-day we are complaining of his aggressiveness.

There is some danger now that the sophisticated will accept the satirist's picture of America, seeing this country, except for their own circle and neighborhood, as all Main Streets, "fronts," East Sides, Y.M. C.A.'s, and the restless rich. Lewis's "Babbitt," with its merciless satire of standardized ambitions, is, I believe, entirely true, but, accepted as an explanation of America, it explains only half. If Mr. Babbitt is America, then Wilson, La Follette, Mrs. Eddy, Hoover, Franklin P. Adams, The Rockefeller Foundation, Edwin Arlington Robinson, the trampers of the High Sierra, the First Expeditionary Force of the War, and Sinclair Lewis himself are well nigh inexplicable. Of course Mr. Lewis did not mean Babbitt to represent America, but that will not prevent the assumption.

If we take Miss Cather's "One of Ours" for our guide, we can at least understand a country which, in the pages of *The Saturday Evening Post,* in the life of its offices and hotels, in its popular amusements and fashionable religions, apparently lives without soul or deeper emotion; for there one finds, as to be fair, one finds in the last chapters of "Babbitt," longing, suffering, hoping humanity pulsating, shrinking, growing under this show of things amidst which it lives. Both books, in my estimation, are valuable as literature, but the second, the volume which is not satire, represents what we have not been taking from the America around us—the vital American not as a type, but as a man who happened to be born in the United States.

I am not, may I pause to explain, endeavoring in this essay to reform American literature. If our better books are becoming by natural process more and more satiric in character, if American writers with brains are choosing types which represent and illustrate America for their characters; well, by all means let us encourage the fashion and see it out. Only a few years ago people were saying that satire of any kind was as rare in American literature as irony, its sharpest instrument. It *is* rare—in the new folk literature of the million-mouthed magazine; but in writing that counts, the somber satire of naturalistic description is common, and the cutting satire of sarcasm and attack certainly not uncommon, especially since the War. If we are to have an age of satire in prose and in verse, let us welcome it; any age in which books are vigorous enough to get an adjective for themselves and their period is to be praised. If necessary, let it be satire, meaty with life and pungent with shrewd reflection, until we have all of us digested what the comic spirit thinks of us and risen wiser, if not happier, men.

That, however, is by no means all, or even the

most, that America has in stock for literature to-day, and this is the point of my essay. Hawthorne looked through his powerful, but narrow, glasses into the lurking-place of New England's moral being. Emerson through his telescopic lens looked at us far away, so far that it was easy to philosophize us. Whitman had bifocals; below he saw us animal, above, by sudden contrast, humans vaster than men. Poe never looked at a man at all in his national or even racial aspects. That unhampered him for art, but takes him out of this consideration. It is irrelevant to call Poe American or Keats English. Mr. Dreiser, and the naturalists who have been following, first, the Russians and Arnold Bennett, then, Joyce and Lawrence, have microscope lenses in their spectacles. They poke their faces close to the object and see too much and too coarsely. And the satiric school glimpses everything on one plane only, like objects seen on the desert at the rise or the set of the sun.

Well and good, and let the fellow who sees to the best purpose be called upon to tell us what he sees. But this does not prevent one from urging that there are discoveries and vast ones waiting the writer who, being neither astigmatic, myopic, nor hypermetropic, looks at us Americans through no glasses at all. He might not see our faults so clearly or so deftly extract that single quality which in each person makes him kin to a group, a class, or a type; but what a relief it would be to feel some quiet and unforced gaze upon us, looking not for essential Americanisms or vices of the industrial order or the results of pioneering or the terrible effect of living in the country *or* the small town *or* the big city *or* New York, but just for human character set in a rich environment! Frost, in his poetry, does a little of this. Masters did once. Are the poets to lead, the prose fictionists to follow?

And character is essentially what the American scene has to offer the makers of literature—character, the essence of the novel (to which plot is only a convenience), the chief ingredient of all literature not lyrical or philosophic. The characters that have escaped description so far in the United States! I know a dozen which, properly interpreted, and transmogrified into art, would be worth all the realistic, erratic, erotic naturalism in a thousand bookshops. Men and women are dying daily who would have made novelists' fortunes and been our delight. Can't we have fewer complexes masquerading as humans, less social conscience, not so many dusty, dirty details of suppressed lives, and more people of blood, gristle, and passion? Can't we have more personality, self-sustained and convincing, which embraces all true motives and impulses, instead of being merely compounded of psychologists' terms? Can't we have men, women, and children whose names we remember although we have known them only in a book? Russian literature will not give them to us, not at least our own brand; nor French, nor British. The job waits upon American writers. Perhaps in serene old age our younger generation will find the time to smile and do it.

What They See in Us

Is it true that materials for literature are lying about waiting to be picked up and built into something? Are there sonnets in subways, novels on the open street, short stories in every crowd, and drama everywhere? If so, it is curious to note what American writers pick up and what they leave by the wayside.

Romance is gathered by truckfuls. Nothing with a rosy gleam to it or the soft feel of sentiment goes unregarded. If a Dakota girl is sent to India as a missionary, or a country boy comes to New York to write; if a corporation lawyer has a melting heart, or his daughter falls in love with a labor leader; if a divorced couple fall in love, or a good-natured boob becomes wealthy by accident, the trifle is snapped up and marketed as fast as typewriter can beat it out into fiction and literary agent send it to the right address.

And what the romanticists leave behind the searchers for sorry realism gather into baskets. They pick up the honeymoon that went stale and the wife who needed more than a husband's love, brush the dust from hard-boiled boyhoods, and cherish the disillusions of the flapper grown up. They collect episodes from the old farm that the romantics never dreamed were happening and favor the anemic and the neurotic, whom red-blooded authors pass over with incomprehension or disgust.

Busiest of all are the humorists. Is there a single aspect of American life, from the funeral to a battle in the Argonne, that has not seemed funny to some one? The romance of courtship, business, adventure, that bubbles in American books like gas in seltzer, seems often to have been pressed into the liquid by the hopeful imagination of the author; but the humor of our life is genuine. It is on the surface, and the American is unfortunate who cannot make a comic strip for himself any day, anywhere.

It is on the surface, and the humorists never look below it. Now come the satirists—Sinclair Lewis, Harry Leon Wilson, Tarkington, Zona Gale (the list is getting long)—and grub for its roots. The chief discoveries about Americans are being made to-day by the satirists. Their notebooks are bulging; never was such a harvest to gather in of the fruits of prosperity, complacency, and a standardized education. The United States, as they make us see ourselves, is one nation-wide satire upon the ideals of Christian civilization, a symbol of all that is egregious, and misguided, and put upon, and boastful, yet also, because it is so vigorous and human, lovable too.

Is this all? Have the romantics and the realists, the satirists and the humorists swept us clean? Is there nothing to sing about in this corner of the world —no chants to be made, no lyric outburst? Are there no thrills in New York except creeps of the flesh?

There seemed to be plenty in England in Shelley's day
and Spenser's. Can you put all of Kansas into a
satire, do up the Rockies by romance, anatomize Chicago by scientific naturalism, or embrace all darkydom
by a laugh? Ladies and gentlemen, you who write
about and around us, there are aspects of America
that you are missing. The country is too rich for you.
The cream of the harvest is going to waste. Ten
thousand things are happening daily whose ultimate
cause is deep under all the hustle and bustle, and may
prove to be one of the rare movements of that sluggish,
powerful creature, human nature itself.

Poetry or prose, it does not matter which, but in
one or the other new discoveries are clamored for. We
are far better represented in general by our writers
than by our Congressmen; but in the emotional interpretation of this busiest and tensest of human ant hills
we are not as yet adequately represented. Wordsworth, in the stale sequel to revolution and hope, called
for a poet, a Milton.

> Milton, thou shouldst be living at this hour.

Neither the epic nor the lyric of modern America
would be a job that Milton could handle, or Dante
either. But some one of powerful imagination whose
feet are free from cumbering detail, with an eye for
wholes, not parts, and the brains of man and the
tongue of angels—well, he would not starve for lack
of readers, even in this rampart of Philistinism and
home of standardized common sense.

A Club Car Homily

OF all melancholy pleasures reading "The New Republic" (not the magazine but Mallock's book, which first advanced the name) is the most complete. There, in the '70s, before the more discontented in this generation were born, are all the modern discontents, all the modern panaceas, all the modern protests against God and atheism, industrialism and the dilettante, tolerance, and the dogmatic. We are children of the nineteenth century still, even though we repudiate Queen Victoria and Mr. Wanamaker!

And yet there is a difference. The passionate struggle between science and religion seems a little ridiculous now, whether read of in "The New Republic" or heard of in Kentucky. Science has conquered the Galilean, as the Galilean was conceived of by the majority in those days. The men and women who read the magazines, travel in trains, stay in hotels, live in the houses of Main Street and Market Street and Lincoln Avenue, show by their lives and their faces that they no longer expect, even by convention, a future life in any way resembling this one. Tacitly, among the so-called civilized, the emphasis has been shifted entirely to this world. Even Catholics have swung to social reform, and no one now consoles the poor for their lack of prosperity by the promise of a certain reward in kind. Social science, which shows us how to get food for all, and biology, which tells us how to digest it, have become our theologies.

There has been, as a result, a decline since the days of "The New Republic," in the objects of our concern. Our faces, here in America especially where we are modernism incarnate, begin to show it. To be advanced, to think for the race is, in practice, to think for health and welfare. The bitter quarrels have shifted from religion to economics. The martyrs are martyrs of social rights. The struggle is to make both minds and bodies equal and give them an equal chance. Conduct is secondary, the will of God is heard of chiefly in sermons and Presidential messages. To the leaders, the contest is as always that of the powers of light against the powers of darkness, but everyday men, everyday Americans particularly, who read so much news that they live in other men's opinions, are let down to a level of materialistic endeavor where success is measured solely in terms of automobiles, income, and reputation.

Sitting in the club car of a cross-country train, looking at the faces—lax, predatory, indifferent, worried, complacent, shrewd, thoughtful, or dull—one knows that all this is true, but knows with even greater certainty that it is not all the truth. For matter, man, spirit, force, and God, whatever they are and whatever terms we apply to them, do not change in their relationship, and our way of handling life is just a passing phase, an experiment like earlier experiments, more successful in some respects, if history can be relied on, less so in others. And yet the materialistic hypothesis, in which speed, comfort, development, control over nature become ends in themselves, has this danger, that the level of thought sinks to the plane of getting things done and made, and stays there.

Perhaps anything else is an illusion; but the men in the club car do not feel so whatever their faces seem to say. The potentiality to be more than a productive machine is implicit in them as it is implicit in their civilization. We cannot turn back the clock of science and its accompanying materialism, and would be fools to do so (if real science, not pseudo-science, is in question) because, however unwise our adjustment to knowledge may be, adjust ourselves we must, and if mechanical living is a price we are paying for a mastery of electricity, thermodynamics, neuroses, and vitamins, it does not follow that we shall always pay in that coin. Science that gave us industrialism with its standardized monotony has already made of the scientist a type that antiquity might envy.

Nor are first impressions true impressions of these machine-made Americans in the club car. To all appearances most of them have been trained to keep doing, keep smiling, taught to say "Thank you" for business reasons, accustomed to converse of nothing that goes deeper than humor or trade. It may be that some of the middle-aged ones are sold to the devil of the commonplace; but not all, especially not youth, or, to pass beyond the club car, women. Questions, impulses, choices, refusals, cravings are hot under that tailored surface which so deceives foreigners, who, finding that American life looks like its advertisements, think that the two are identical. The difficulty is to bring into the stream of national consciousness, which concerns itself now with production, the thoughts and emotions which characterize man awake and alive.

That is a job for literature, for poetry by choice, which has of late taken everyday America for its topic, and plunged after its subject into the commonplace. While it is true that literature follows life, it is equally true that life follows literature. An emotion powerfully struck off in poetry breeds its like in a thousand readers. Indeed, if the warm emotions and philosophic thinking which still function beneath the crust of business-as-usual are not to atrophy as being activities not required for commercial efficiency, the arts, but particularly literature, must come to the rescue. Fiction in the United States, and especially the short story, is trying to reconcile man to a mechanical environment by telling him fairy tales of escape from it all by quick wealth or sudden love. What the age—no, not clamors for, since it would be as likely to clamor for castor oil and mustard plaster—what the age very evidently needs is poetry and fiction that shall awaken the dormant life of the emotions in club cars, offices, factories, homes before it weakens into feeble sentiment or is lost in efficient dullness.

American Style

We have set no standard of literary American prose, in spite of our distinctively American way of writing. The best American prose is being written by the busiest American writers, too busy, perhaps unfortunately, to bother about standards. Those who do talk about standards, talk moonshine. Their conception of fine prose is drawn from De Quincey or Hazlitt, Ruskin or Lamb. They would have an American speak Oxford English. Their grandfathers complained of Abraham Lincoln because he was so little like a British Premier. They criticize as "journalese" the native writing, which is without doubt or question the groundwork of American literary prose.

American prose can best be studied in the newspapers and magazines. When it is good enough to have qualities worth discussing, they are different from the British. It has a different rhythm; it is more staccato; less rich in figures; more inclined to familiar colloquialism; more practical in sound and effect. When it tries to be literary in the English sense it becomes rhetorical and imitative. At its best it is never reminiscent, seldom allusive, always quick and nervous. Its success lies in epithet and antithesis, hardly ever in atmosphere and flow. It is a prose formed by journalists who have written steadily for

a mass instead of a class of readers. They have borrowed the informality of the stump speech and the
eager emphasis of quick conversation.   There are
other and more subtle differences from British
examples and practice, but all the most important are
in kind and not in degree.

Grant this last and it is easier to ask without mis-
understanding for a beautiful prose that is distinctly
American. This flexible journalists' prose of ours has
all the desirable qualities except beauty. It has been
made adequate to the expression of everything in
every-day America except beauty. It is sheer nonsense to say that this is because there is no beauty in
American living. The best beauty here is different,
as we are different, and harder to catch in prose because more novel and deceptive in its manifestations.
Perhaps there is less of it—that is a matter of opinion
—but it is as real as we are. Our novelists have been
letting contemporary beauty, like a mill stream loose,
run through their gates while they have been senti-
mentalizing us or exposing our ugliness. The journalists have been too hurried for beauty—not too hurried
in their writing, but in their perceptions and reflections. They have had too much sense to put beauty
on their prose, like an opera cloak on a working dress,
and so have escaped becoming little Lambs or near
Ruskins; that has been left to the milder essayists and
writers of club papers. Our good prose borrows no
beauty, but might well create it.

All this will be manifest when the writer, or group

of writers, appears in due course, and takes this familiar journalists' style of ours—the stone that the *literati* rejected—and builds upon it an edifice for beauty as well as for use. Then we will make anthologies of American prose in which many a casual paragraph or hasty article of many a supposedly unliterary writer of to-day will find place as precursors of the prose of X, excelling it in freshness and spontaneity, although lacking the splendor of phrase and vigor of rhythm which came with the sudden flowering of American Literary genius in the year ——.

In the meantime, does no one on this side of the Atlantic dare to write beautifully? Is there no one who finds beauty in American experience and can put it into words? Why is ugliness fashionable? Is it because this was the only escape from prettiness, which has been our ideal of beauty in literature? Haven't we eaten our peck of ugliness—and more? Will no one say, I see new beauty and will make my old typewriter express it! We have an American style, with all the tongues except the tongue of flame.

Critics from Abroad

THE American, says D. H. Lawrence in his "Classic American Literature," is shaping in secret a new character which is an effect of his new environment. The spirit of Place, a kind of Indian demon, is working upon his subconscious mind, producing the great American grouch, "the Orestes-like frenzy of restlessness," "the inner malaise," which are his characteristic attributes. And what, Mr. Lawrence, is the effect of this spirit of Place upon visiting Englishmen? That He, She, or It makes the native restless and grouchy may, or may not, be true, but the spell cast by something in our environment upon distinguished visitors from abroad is unmistakable.

The French who came over with Lafayette were troubled about our manners. Traveling Englishwomen of the mid-nineteenth century were sure that our morals were degenerating. Towards the end of the century every departing journalist and statesman left behind him a little homily on our gross materialism. And now the migrant flight of British novelists, essayists, and poets that visits us annually is deeply concerned for the American mind as it displays itself in literature. We are too shallow, too smart, too superficial, too something else. We lack seriousness, finish, elegance, what not. And the American academic world echoes.

Granted that American literature is too, too something or another, and utterly lacking in what not, why are our visitors so sententious about it? Even when known as humorists in their native land, they break, within twenty-four hours of landing, into wise saws upon Art, Literature, and Life. They act precisely like a Parent asked to say a few words to the boys at school. And they become dogmatic. The genial Hilaire Belloc was willing to argue the essential difference between everything English and American, even with St. Paul's Church under his nose and Mr. Christopher Morley standing beside him. Arnold Bennett could see nothing but architecture in America. Mr. Wells lectured us daily when here upon a thesis which he had prepared five years in advance of his landing. Mr. Lawrence has divided our souls into two parts, and described each part accurately.

Curious also the air of responsibility which these visitors suck from our atmosphere and grow great by. There is an anxious solicitude in their form of address—never "America's this or that," or "American," but "your markets," "your books," "your taste," as if the United States had one neck to be twisted and one rear to be spanked. No one of light and learning from the other side has discharged his solemn duty to civilization until he has given tender and solicitous advice to youthful America.

Did you ever hear Americans bewailing in the daily

papers the state of letters in France? Or being inter-viewed upon the hope of the British novel? Or lec-turing in Great Britain upon the revival of British poetry? Is it because they are incapable, or can find nothing to criticize? They are loud enough upon the merits or demerits of a novel or a poem, French or British; but apparently they never feel the inner urge to save Europe from the effects of maturity. It takes our atmosphere to arouse the Sir Oracle dormant in every one. The lightness and clarity of our air pro-duce a certain dizziness in the British mind which dis-charges in rebuke, advice, and prophecy. Westing has always this effect upon minds sprung from European culture. New Yorkers in San Francisco behave like Englishmen in New York. They grow sententious, ad-visory, and sometimes patronizing, although proximity to the ancient East keeps them from being too absurd.

It is a subtle demon, this spirit of Place. Having made preachers of our visiting artists it proceeds to fuddle them. Kipling tried to write like Bret Harte; Stevenson imitated Hawthorne; H. G. Wells will never be plain Mr. Britling again; and here is Mr. Lawrence, in the book already mentioned, writing in the staccato style developed by Mr. Hearst's newspapers and get-ting badly mixed now and then in his American slang. The American environment has given his fine prose a case of the Arizona blues.

The truth is that American literature is too much talked about and not enough read, at least by Euro-peans and American professors of English. What the sincere American artist needs is not advice but a hearing. And visiting critics should resist the impulse to tell America all about herself. It is an old Indian demon tempting them to speak in advance of knowledge.

III

Sex and the Censorship

Sex in Fiction

In 1800 fiction was charged with infidelity; in 1830 it was accused of frivolity; in 1890 it was suspected of immorality; in the 1920's it is freely convicted of too much sex. Thus in every age some complaint against the novel, or that acted fiction we call drama, becomes a convention. For many worthy Americans to-day "sex drama" and "sex novel" are not definitions, but terms of abuse intended to settle the matter, just as for a certain type of mind "radical" as a descriptive epithet ends discussion.

Well, if fiction goes in for sex more thoroughly now than in the past there must be a reason, and it is idle to begin campaigns against passional or outspoken fiction until that reason is disengaged from prejudice and obscurity. Upon the results of such an inquiry hang the answers to such elementary questions as, How much sex should go into fiction? and, How frankly should sex in fiction be expressed? questions so naïvely simple that they have gone unanswered while controversy raged. Readers have been shocked or disgusted, writers have been truculently candid or defiantly obscene, ethics and instinct have been in debate, epithets have been hurled, criticism has been feverish; definition has never had a chance. I suppose we know what we mean by fiction, but do we comprehend its necessary relations in any given period to sex?

If sex is the distinguishing feature of the novel of the 1920's, it is easy to find the reason. Literature has generally followed or paralleled philosophy, probably because both mirror the prevailing temperament of life. Discoveries or theories which affect philosophy come out in literature shortly afterward, like a rash. Scholastic philosophy interpenetrates the medieval romance. The renaissance of classic thinking was reflected in the literature of humanism. Deism had its poetry and prose. Darwinism is a postulate for the discussion of nineteenth-century literature in the latter half. But the fact is self-evident and needs no tedious exposition.

Now the relativity of Einstein may influence our philosophy of life profoundly before we have finished absorbing it; so far, however, it is a little remote from the science of human nature, and fiction is unaware of it. Not so with the new psychology of sex complexes and repressions. That began with sex abnormalities as a means of discovering the truth about sex, and passed almost immediately out of cold science into warm debate and quick philosophizing. Concurrently, biology stepped onward with its rediscovery of Mendelism, and made reproduction, as the key to heredity, the center of its problem; and this also came to the public ear. Thus the popular philosophy of the day, by which I mean the philosophy of life which seems warm and vital to the layman, is largely built upon questions of sex. It is inconceivable that literature, even without the moral oversets of war, would not be powerfully affected.

Knowledge, and therefore consciousness, of sex has greatly increased. The Elizabethans knew that love colored the world for the lover; but what they knew experientially and metaphysically we begin to know by symptom and its cause. We can trace the negatives as well as the positives of love—the effects of repression, the share of instinct, the results in time as well as in space. Shakespeare depicted man in love more vividly than the modern psychologists, but they have ticketed love's remote, unsuspected effects. They have carried their analysis beyond and before adolescence, and traced love's pathology as well as its healthy function. In scope and detail we have more knowledge if not more wisdom in sex. And feminism has doubled interest in the question, for the female sex has now a different environment of custom, new sets of activities, and a different emphasis in discussion. Women raise problems now which once were allocated only to man. No wonder that those for whom sex is still a moral question solely and those for whom it is at present merely a problem in psychology have difficulty in understanding each other. They do not speak the same language. Never before, at least never since the first Christian centuries, have there been such divergent opinions in a single civilization as to the status of sex. And this tension of opinions also finds its way into literature.

Much that is being written in science or pseudo-science to-day is still stamped by the Freudian emphasis upon abnormality. Much of it deals with hypotheses unproved. Nevertheless, there is enough ready for acceptance (which, indeed, merely explains what good sense has long apprehended) to give the literary imagination material to feed upon. "Advanced" writers, and many who are never called "advanced," are well aware of this material, have let, indeed, their imaginations too often run dangerously ahead of science. Sex as a natural force contributory to all the emotions is familiar to them, and so is sex repressed or diverted and become a malady. Novelists are thinking of sex for itself and as itself, which does not necessarily mean that they have ceased to think also of sex in terms of morality. And as they think, so they write. The youth who discusses coldly topics upon which age is warmly reticent has become a commonplace of satire.

Therefore at a moment of such intense interest it is clearly ridiculous to criticize fiction for dealing with sex, or to talk about sex dramas and sex novels as if the presence of such an interest made them evil. Is it likely that writers will keep sex out of fiction just as they are made aware in detail, instead of by intuition, how sex permeates every act and thought of the living organism? Or that we, the readers, will agree to deplore its presence there? Can sex ever be kept out of fiction? If you choke it back in one direction, it rises in another. If you discourage its normal expression,

you get, on the one hand, erotic adventures and super-
subtle analyses, and, on the other, movie melodrama
of the caveman and strained innocence, or squashy
novels of facile emotions. Love complexes are not confined to the perverted or the abnormal; they determine sentimentality also and the mawkish emotion of
purity that protests too much. The complaint, in a
time like this one, cannot be of sex; it can only be of
sex in exaggeration. The division which our amateur
censors make between sex and non-sex novels is a false
one; it should be between stories of sex in proportion
and sex out of proportion. This is a distinction which
bears some relation to reality, and is valuable in the
criticism of art.

Even the most prudent reader must by now be
familiar with novels of sex out of proportion. Let me
rudely classify them for him into the behavioristic, the
phallic, the neurotic, and the stereotyped varieties.
Sex in proportion may be left for a later page.

Some novelists are interested in human behavior for
its emotional values, just as some psychologists are interested in behavior for its scientific values. Such a
novelist seldom bothers about plot. If he is Mr.
Aldous Huxley, writing "Crome Yellow," he tosses
together half a dozen of his contemporaries in an
imagined house party and lets them talk and act the
sex that is in them. The distinguishing feature of
each is his or her sex complex (they all have them,
negative or positive). Nothing important happens;

only some brilliant conversation and a few emotional episodes, and the story floats and sails upon the turbid intensity of restless sex. Or she, if it is Miss Rose Macaulay in "Dangerous Ages," fixes her attention upon the difference in sex reactions among the young, the middle-aged, the old, and pursues an investigation of jealousy complexes and the transmutation of sex power into some other kind of energy. She is clever, original, observant, but this is the sum of her rather delightful book. Or, there is Miss May Sinclair's "Life and Death of Harriett Frean," which follows the so-called parent complex through all its deadly course, so that in the story of poor Harriett the behavior of warped sex is the only theme. These are all interesting books, Miss Sinclair's perfect of its kind, though its kind is a miniature, Mr. Huxley's rich in pointed flippancy, Miss Macaulay's full of shrewd insight. Nevertheless, they are specialists' work, essays in sex rather than stories, examples of the novel made narrowly experimental by an over-emphasis upon the behavior of sex. Their characters are like puppets that all dance to tugs from a single direction.

The phallic novels of our day also illustrate disproportion. Mr. Lawrence's books, of which I have written elsewhere, are powerful in this genre, and contain admirable qualities which this definition does not touch. My point is that. in his novels, and in the stories of, let us say, Waldo Frank or Ben Hecht in this country, the urgency of sex is so immediate in every thought and action that the thing becomes an obsession. The genre has reached its climax in the "Ulysses" of James Joyce, an extravaganza of erratic genius in which literally scores of pages are driven into an extravagant indecency by an obsession with inflamed or perverted sex that hurries the author away from proportion, away from coherence, and very far away from art. Subtle studies result, but also an emotional intensifying of life which is often wearisome and sometimes distressing. The phallic novel at its worst is no more valuable as a transcript of life in the round than a study of dipsomaniacs in a private sanatorium.

Then there is the neurotic novel, where "change partners" is the command in every other chapter, where every one is restless, aimless, unsatisfied, and a complicated series of strains and tensions makes the story. Sick sex is usually the cause. The characters, even the most amusing, like some of Scott Fitzgerald's, are sick from frustration or satiety. They are slaves to longing, like Hergesheimer's Lee Brandon, or hopeless or helpless or shameless. The effect is like conversation over an undercurrent of nervous music. No one may enter these stories who has not a complex; and here Freud is justified: the complex is always of sex.

And last, to sweep ten thousand volumes into a single category, are those stereotyped stories which express not quality, but quantity of sex. I mean the popular narrative of blatant innocence in which the kiss that begins upon the slip cover is held with brief intermissions throughout the volume; where there is constant amorous emotion, and a surfeit of pulchritudinous femininity and excessively masculine men. Harmless these books may be, except to taste, but they are just as out of proportion in sex as the sophisticated studies of behavior described above; and if Lawrence and Huxley give only partial truth, these are not true at all, except to the desire of feeble imaginations too timid to be wicked and too weak to be sanely good.

The stereotype of sex has been done in every generation. Shakespeare was often guilty; so, I think, was Fielding sometimes, who, it must be remembered, did not confine his studies to Tom Jones. The neurotic, the phallic, and the behavioristic books, however, are essentially modern; the sex in them is a product of the modern temperament and modern nerves, and is illuminated and influenced in its creation by a science which did not exist before the nineteenth century.

But that these ill proportioned novels are typically modern is no proof that they are intrinsically excellent. Most of them are more interesting as phenomena than valuable as permanent art. They are not, as reckless critics charge, decadent; they are experimental. And it is hardly worth while to attack the stronger writers, like Mr. Lawrence, for indecency. These men are sincere artists. If they are bold in their statements, it is not to be naughty; it is because they believe candor to be essential to their project, which is to imitate and interpret and satirize what they see in life. They mirror their times as did the Restoration drama and the French literature of the *régence*, and probably catch about as much in their glass and miss as much. Mr. Lawrence sees the world in terms of sex, precisely as single-taxers see it in terms of land, socialists in terms of unearned increment, and writers of movie-scenarios in terms of heart interest and violent sensation. There was sure to be a literature of sex in this generation, there was sure to be an overplus of sex for a while in our fiction, and we are lucky to have a few writers who have written brilliantly under its influence. But an overplus of sex is like any other overplus: it brings reaction with it. Nemesis awaited the tearful fiction of our ancestors, and Nemesis, perhaps a distant one, awaits Mr. Lawrence. Like many an extinct animal, he has specialized too far.

Shall we urge going back, then, to some earlier, simpler condition, where sex, instead of an irritant, was an impulse, and men and women, instead of having complexes, were merely virtuous or sinners? Impossible; we cannot go back. Whatever may have been true of the past, the fringe of civilization has now passed beyond the point where virtue may be defined as obeying the rules, and transgression called a venial sin to be retrieved by penitence and flagellation. Now that we know how complex in their ramifications of influence are the sex relations between man and woman, we must go forward, not resting upon the ethics of a simpler period, nor yet discarding the Christian moral code, but rather, as has been done a hundred times before, endeavoring to tame without repression the turbulence of sex to the requirements of a good civilization.

Perhaps the books I have been discussing are the first steps in such a process. Their stories of strain and warp and desire present the sex maladjustments of the day; and doubtless that is a great service to the intellect, if not always to art. They are novels of maladjustment—maladjustment of knowledge to tradition and experience. And some of them betray an indigestion of dubious information, and others the shell-shock of social groups shaken and relaxed by war.

But as we cannot keep sex out of our fiction, so we cannot wait to write until the new psychology has made love into a formula. Of course it never will; at the most it will reveal a little more fully what love does to the nervous organism. In the meantime we shall continue to make novels, and as complexes become more familiar, and society adjusts itself to new conditions, even the more violent may recover their balance, and keep sex in proportion.

I am aware that I have been using a formula myself throughout this essay, and I am quite willing to drop the matter in hand for a moment to defend formulas—in proportion. When Milton attacked Salmacius, when Coleridge and Wordsworth attacked the Augustans, when Arnold used up the Philistines, when Poe redefined poetry, and when Mr. Spingarn issued a manifesto against Paul Elmer More, they merely substituted one formula for another. There is nothing objectionable in formulas so long as they remain working theories of truth and are not allowed to crystallize into the ultimate truth itself. I have spoken of sex out of proportion, which is not so much a formula as an accusation; and I have spoken of sex in proportion, which *is* a formula, without defining it. I am quite willing to say what I mean, but with the definite proviso that it is a living ideal I am defining, which, like life, is subject to adaptation and evolution. Sex in proportion as a formula for 1840 is by no means the same as sex in proportion for 1940. At best one can only say what it might very well mean to-day; but if said honestly and with reference to the needs of art rather than to the teaching of morality, that may be worth saying.

I do not believe that any writer upon sex can keep it in proportion to life as it is best and most vividly lived if he is not keenly aware of standards of decency and morality where they in their turn are most delicately and truly apprehended. This sounds delightfully old-fashioned, but may be true despite that.

Decency is a matter of taste. Decency lies always somewhere between prudishness and the shocking. As the least unsophisticated are aware, what shocks one generation does not shock another. Knees, for example, have run the whole scale from inevitable through invisible to permissible. And it is equally true that prudishness, which lurks in all sex morality, although it is in no sense a part of it, has also advanced and retreated. Prudishness in fiction is not to be taken with the seriousness which the emancipated young bestow upon it. There are masterpieces of prudishness, like "Cranford," that literature could not do without. It is annoying only when it rasps upon taste, which is irritated by repressions, naïve hypocrisies, and moral snobberies precisely as a man of taste suffers from stiff mannerisms and tyrannies of a conventional social code. And it is taste rather than morality which suffers from indecency in fiction. I do not deny that "suggestive" fiction has its effect upon the susceptible mind; but "suggestive" fiction is seldom indecent, although often immoral. Its authors are much too clever to risk plain statement. The indecency of the modern realist is more likely to encourage strict living out of sheer reaction against the ugliness of depicted vice. It is usually honest in its intent, and its prime offense is against good taste.

I maintain, then, that the great novelist will seldom be troubled by questions of decency or indecency. He will make decency, for his taste will be a register of the susceptibilities of his age. Knees will be knees to him, and neither non-existent nor means of provocation. If he beskirts them, it is for cause; and if he frees them, it is a sign not of immorality, but that dressing is different. If he writes of knees instead of souls and hearts and brains, the probabilities are that he is not great.

As for morality, in the monastic period of the Middle Ages, and again in the nineteenth century, as the meaning put upon the word indicated, it centered in sex. At present sex is being affiliated not so much with morals as with behavior. Whether it makes you healthy, wealthy, and wise is to be the criterion of your control of sex. Thus we have passed from one overemphasis to another, particularly in our criticism and our fiction.

I certainly do not wish to enter upon anything so difficult as a definition of morality. But here is a salient fact: whether you derive your moral principles from a definite code laid down in sacred writ and the doctrine of the churches, or whether you conceive of morality as a deduction from the experience of the race for its proper guidance, the result is pretty much the same when it comes to judging really vital instances. The action permitted may be different,—divorce may be forbidden or encouraged,—but the responsibility of man for woman and of woman for man works out about the same by either system.

I refuse to estimate a novelist by his attitude toward divorce, but I am quite willing to judge him by his fundamental moral attitude. Lacking stability here, he may be almost anything but sound, and therefore almost anything but great. But I will have no petty formulas of morality to judge him by. As knees do not disqualify him, so ethical practices which belong to his own time rather than ours do not disqualify him.

Chaucer is indecent, but morally sound. I will not condemn Stendhal because his moral attitude differs from my own.

Of course a fundamentally immoral writer is a rare bird. The novelist is more likely to err in his sense of proportion. Especially is he prone, like D. H. Lawrence, to let sex and its problems run away with him until it warps his moral universe, until sex (or money or success or cleverness) becomes more important than the life of which it is a part. Scott's novels boil down to an essential Toryism, if you let all their delightful romance and sound sense bubble away; Dickens distils into a rather soapy humanitarianism, if you are silly enough to vaporize his wonderful people; but the much less considerable narrative of the over-sexed novel evaporates of itself and leaves only a protest or an obsession.

Novelists, great and small, must keep their heads in this rather startling period. If sex means anything to them (and otherwise they are not novelists), they must keep up with the baggage and yet not surrender to her wiles. They must realize that sex is creative energy, and instead of playing variations upon sensuality or making investigations in the pathological, they must study the whole man or woman. This means that there can be no rigid interpretation of the formula, sex in proportion. Sex moves and creates and destroys in all of us, but in different measure; and the measure for the novelist depends upon the total significance of his scene and upon his own sensibilities.

Mr. Tarkington and Mr. Galsworthy, for example, give us marvelously different views of the human animal regarded as gender, and yet usually succeed in keeping sex in proportion.

Tarkington has the normal American attitude toward sex. His heroes and heroines control their sex; or, if they fail to do so, it is outside of the story. One sees the results and sometimes is shown the cause, but the circumstances do not interest the novelist or his readers, which is perhaps unfortunate. And yet this does not mean that Mr. Tarkington is ignorant or hypocritical or suppressed as regards sex. "Alice Adams" will convince a discerning reader that he knows more of the curious pranks of the instinct within us than many a younger writer who may have created neurotics in order to display his knowledge of Freud. Sex for Mr. Tarkington is important only in its more romantic and more humorous manifestations. He keeps it in proportion to his purpose, which is the gently satiric study of American experience.

Mr. Galsworthy is different. He is an artist with a social conscience, not a humorist. His studies of human nature have more depth and breadth to them than Mr. Tarkington's, although they are not more discriminating or more true. But his novels constantly spread toward that area of life where sex dominates. In "The Forsyte Saga" his crises are substantially all of them crises of sex. Like D. H. Lawrence,

he keeps the sex urge dominant through every ramifica-
tion of plot. And yet in this remarkable chain of stories, sex, although dominant, is in proportion. One can
describe the "Saga" as a symbolic study of the Philis-
tine, and be reasonably correct. The London of the
Forsytes is as solid and as varied and as versatile,
though not so humorous, as the London of "Vanity
Fair." If Irene, with her fatal gift of potent sex, is
the key which unlocks the plot and the symbol which
gives it meaning, she and the sex impulses and nega-
tions which complement her influence do not drive the
rest of life from the story. There is more sex in "The
Forsyte Saga" than lies within Tarkington's sympathies and discernments, but it is sex in proportion.

Viewed this way, the whole question, whether for
moralists or critics of art, becomes, I will not say simple, but a problem where judgment instead of prejudice can be applied, and discriminations be exercised.
It is possible to appreciate the genius of some of the
bad boys of literature while deprecating their taste.
It is possible to praise a passionate sex interest without forswearing morality. It is possible to condemn an
obsession by sex without believing that "sex story" is
a synonym for something bad.

And is it not more than probable that a historian,
standing without this hurly-burly and viewing it critically, would say of our new discoveries in sex, and
the disturbance of social customs which the age of
feminism and the break-up of nineteenth century discipline have brought about—would he not say that a

great surge of creative energy was in process of release; that already it has had its prophets, its persecutors, its victims, and its slaves? That it requires, as human impulses always do, not suppression, but direction and mastery? I think that he would, and I hope that we shall hear less and less of sex as a term of disapproval, and see more and more of the breadth of sex influence reflected in art, and in its true proportions. Let us have Chaucer rather than Longfellow, Rabelais rather than Mabie, Sterne rather than Harold Bell Wright, if we must make a choice; but, better still, men as great or greater who can give final expressions to sex and yet keep it in proportion.

Censorship

THE objection is not to censorship, it is to the censors; it is not to the principle that certain things should be forbidden on the stage and screen and in books, it is to the way in which any law establishing censorship is sure to be administered. Good table manners are desirable and foul ones deplorable, but if censors should be appointed over the conduct of spoons, forks, knives, and plates no left-handed man would be safe and questions of manners would become questions of etiquette. In religion Archbishop Laud and the Grand Inquisitor were censors. We do not wish to see again individuals vested with their arbitrary powers over custom and belief.

Arbitrary power over the morals of literature is almost equally obnoxious. Few individuals are fit to assume it, and they would never take or be given the job. For the power to censor undoubtedly warps the mind of the censorer. If he has a hidden sensitiveness to aspects of indecency or vice—and who has not?—it will be quickened and result in violent reactions, which sooner or later will unseat his judgment, making him partial or vindictive, prying, suspicious, or obtuse. Furthermore, an effective censorship demands a consistency so delicate and exact as to appear inconsistent. Indecency is not absolute—it is relative; and whether it is censorable depends upon a dozen factors, of which audience, tone, occasion, and effect are some. If we are to weed out all the naughtiness, all the frankness, all the earthly wit and gross humor from literature, we should also provide readers without sex. An ideal censor should have a moral sense, an esthetic sense, and a sense of humor, all of the acutest, with common sense to govern them, and a deep-going knowledge of human nature behind. Where is the man, and how long would he retain his necessary and exquisite balance if given arbitrary power and driven by officious meddlers to exercise it?

The principle of criticism by planes is applicable to these vexing questions of morality in literature. The morality or the immorality of a book is partly to be determined by the purpose of the author and partly by conformity or non-conformity to the ethics of the civilization that produces it. Let the first be decided before argument begins upon the second. It is intolerable that an attempt to expose evil should be subject to the same law that condemns the book which fosters vice. As for decency in books and plays, it is often a question of taste and still more often determined by the context. A word that is rankly indecent in a comic scene may bear the moral grandeur of Isaiah himself upon a different occasion. Are censors to decide?

The truth is that in ethics we are a lazy and fearful generation and show our weakness by appointing dictators to act for us. It is, of course, a period of

rapidly changing social conditions, the country drift-
ing to the towns, transportation made easy, the clutch
of environment upon the individual loosened, a period
of disturbing revelations by science which have confused our sense of right conduct, all emphasized by the
relaxations and reactions of a vast war. Indignantly
we see change occurring visibly all about, some of it
for the worse, and all of it different, and helplessly
call the police to distinguish between wrong and right.
But the finer shades of right and wrong in these delicate matters are difficult to discover. It is the public,
by public opinion, that must protect itself when good
and possible evil are mixed, which is the case in the
really important instances where censorship would
have to decide.

The courts, it seems to us, are infinitely preferable
to arbitrary censorship as a check upon pornography
and commercialized lust. In the courts argument is
possible and a trained judicial intelligence can weigh
the case. The functions of prosecutor and judge are
not combined. And if an informal body could be
constituted, made up of those responsible for production and distribution of books and plays—a body, let
us say, of publishers, managers, booksellers, authors;
and if this body had advisory power, so that reference
might be made to it of doubtful cases before the law
was risked or invoked, why then we might expect a
greater degree of intelligence in action—more really
bad books and bad plays suppressed before birth, fewer
instances of reckless accusation, freedom for writers

within limits which their own public opinion would lay down.

Not that all this would settle the question of clean literature. How can it be settled until we all agree upon what we mean by "clean," which will only be when the human intellect is standardized into dead uniformity? It is not possible and it is not desirable to settle the question once for all, since each new case may rouse a new query. But we may force ourselves and the public generally to be more intelligent and more responsible if we refuse to delegate our moral sense to the censors, with power to act as they see fit.

Sterilizing Literature

THE quarrel over morality in literature is like most acrimonious quarrels—the participants are most of them partly wrong and partly right, and so can agree upon nothing. The reformers want pure literature; the literary guild and most readers who call themselves literary want good literature; the creative writer who needs room to pioneer in the study of human nature wants true literature; and the purveyor of sensation and pimp of sensuality wants to turn pornography into cash. The first three groups are agreed in their detestation of the fourth, but they differ sadly as to what is purity, what is truth, and what is excellence in literature.

Now, it is not necessary to invoke a censorship to suppress an immoral book, in which plot and incident are definitely contrived for an immoral purpose; the law already provides a penalty for such a book. But some would go further. They would have a book that is anywhere indecent or "disgusting" suppressed without reference either to its value as a whole or the intent of the writer. It is needless to say that an honest jury charged with such a law would have to suppress the Old Testament, which, without reference to its purpose or its value as a whole, is certainly indecent in parts; would have to rule out most of

Shakespeare, Sterne, Swift, Fielding, Smollett, Chaucer, Congreve, and much of Byron, Swinburne, Shelley, and other names as great. The innocent would go down with the guilty by such a law, and a literary masterpiece would have to be judged not by its excellence or by its intent, but solely by the taste or the reticence of its author. And "decency" and "disgusting" are both relative terms, defined largely by the conventions of the period of the controversy. We marvel at the friends of Goldsmith who were disgusted by his characters from the lower ranks of society; they would marvel at some of our standards of decency in conversation.

However, we do not much fear such a law, for its own unwisdom would in practice break it down. What we do fear is the tendency to sap responsibility by legislation. No one denies the danger of lewd literature; and no sensible person should deny the problem raised by frank literature. The analogy with the problem of diet is exact. Pickles are said not to be good for young girls, cold milk is certainly bad for babies, the sausage in the mouth of the four-year-old on Macdougal Street is assuredly a menace to his internals. But are you going to regulate diet by law and censorship? The law forbids food that is poisonous for everybody, but to pass a statute against overfeeding infants or underfeeding adolescence is to carry paternalism to absurdity. Have we come to a point where all responsibility is to be taken from parents, librarians, and individuals themselves? Do we want a Volstead Act in literature which forbids not merely the alcohol, but the very bubbles in literature, for fear youth will get indigestion from drinking ginger ale?   You simply cannot overprotect from any chance blast of ugly knowledge or profane mirth without sterilizing literature and emasculating the reader.   Books clearly immoral in purpose and books intended to be sensually suggestive should be and can be suppressed; but when the question of moral values is doubtful, or when it is not a question of moral values at all, but of standards of taste and frankness in language, the purpose of the author being beauty, truth, or revelation, then readers, critics, publishers, and distributers must be their own judges and exercise their own censorship by private judgment and public opinion.   Anything else will give the Dogberries and Shallows their opportunity and will lead to penalizing originality, while in the turmoil vice goes free.   And as for the pure, the true, and the good in literature, the reader who seeks the truest books will usually find that they are the best; and the best writers will quite generally possess that purity of purpose which is a hundred times more pure than the frigid inoffensiveness of a sterile book that calls no unpleasant thing by name.

Privately Printed

WHAT are we to say of the privately printed book; the racy book, published in a limited edition at an unlimited price, for readers supposed to be old enough to take care of themselves? The moralists suspect the privately printed book of pandering; some editors agree with them; the publishers indignantly deny all but the loftiest motives. What is the truth?

The truth is that while "privately printed," like "sterling" or "union made" or any other label, has been fraudulently used, the principle involved is much more important than the occasional evasion.

You may believe that good books must treat only of the sweet, the pure, the lovely, and the good, no matter what real life may be like. Or you may think that morality, ethics, decency, and the social virtues generally have nothing to do with art, and that the only question that can be applied to books is, "Are they well or badly done?" Or you may insist that literature (both artistic and scientific) be submitted to exactly the same moral restrictions which we apply to life; namely, that a book is subject to official reproval only if it inflicts damage upon the community in an actionable sense.

Now, if you believe as many honest people do, that books which do not uplift are unworthy, then your judgment of art is warped in the trunk and we will not hear you. If you believe, as many profess to believe, that the products of art and science have no relation whatsoever to morality, then we will know that you are indifferent to social needs and refuse your critical guidance. But even if you avoid these heresies the subject is difficult.

For let us assume three typical cases: The first is a novel of excellent art and honest truth which deals, let us say, almost exclusively with the complexes of sex and the subways of erotic emotion, literally, though perhaps not lasciviously, described. The second is a narrative of amorous adventure, unmoral and indecent, but salted with such wit and so shrewdly reflective upon weak human nature as to delight the sophisticated mind. And the third shall be a so-called classic, of indubitable literary and historical worth, but gross with the libertinism of a decadent age, and thoroughly immoral in its philosophy.

Shall these three books be published and printed freely in English as they readily may be in French? Or shall they be suppressed? Or shall they be printed for those who will have at least as much appreciation of their art as of their lewdness or their erotic exposures?

If there is such a thing as moral democracy, then all men should have an equal opportunity to corrupt their minds with wicked books. Such an ideal of democracy will not win many admirers. You can write of good books and bad books in the artistic sense of the adjectives, but when Mr. Sumner or any one else speaks of books good *for,* or or books bad *for,* in the moral sense of the words, he cannot mean good or bad for the whole democracy without talking nonsense. A book is not bread that tastes alike to all men, it is a stimulant or a depressive, a food or a poison, a tonic or a corrosive, according to circumstances. Exceptions we will make, of course, for books whose purpose is merely salacious, which are lewd without art, or frank without real truth. Such books the penal code provides for. But where there is real merit the question of expediency is instantly complicated by the need to know who are the readers and why they will read. It is the distinction between the scribbling on the lavatory wall, foul and intended for the foul minded, and the dance of the seven veils, the *grosseries* of Rabelais, or the satire of the Romans, where beauty, wit, or power are coördinate with incitements to the flesh.

This is the argument for the privately printed book and the limited edition. It is the argument for special magazines and for a freedom for *The Dial* that could not wisely be permitted to *The Saturday Evening Post.* And such a defense is very necessary, because among obscene books it is invariably the work of artistic power that is chosen for persecution. Vulgar mediocrity on the stage and elsewhere escapes, while too outspoken genius is suppressed. The energy that might stamp out the dirty postcard and the vile pamphlet is devoted to saving the great democracy from books they could not understand and would neither see nor hear of, unless advertised by martyrdom.

But private printing, as authors know, is one of the worst methods of issuing a book. It is a sign usually of weakness in the book, distrust of the reader, or fear of the hand of authority. Responsibility should rest, where it belongs, with the publisher, who should affix his name to the book. If he is reputable he is worthy of trust; and it is in his province to decide what books shall be published and for whom. By the character of his advertising he can direct a book to its proper market, and if he fails in his judgment or duty public opinion can reach and punish him with ease. The idea of a lay jury to pass on manuscripts before publication is ridiculous. Only doubtful and difficult cases would be passed on to such a tribunal, and if the jurors ever should agree upon an important decision, they would in all probability be wrong.

Crazy Literature

THE human race is but doubtfully and unsteadily sane, clinging to normality as much by inertia as by will, and constantly swinging towards eccentricity or the inane, while individuals are flung off on either side into sheer insanity or the idiotic. So it is with man's literature. Whole movements and periods are slightly insane, as were perhaps the metaphysical school of the seventeenth century and the Euphuists; and men of vivid but unsteady genius or weaklings of brittle intellect are tossed across the line. Crazy literature is not necessarily bad literature; sometimes, as with Blake and Nietzsche, it may show signs of recurrent insanity and yet be of extraordinary value, but it is highly important that we should know when it is unbalanced and why. To mistake insanity for genius, or to fail to distinguish between the insanity and the greatness in a man who is not altogether sane, is to risk futilities of criticism and absurdities in imitation and praise.

A wave towards insanity in literature usually follows upon some great discovery in philosophy or innovation in religion. It springs from what the psychologists call an obsession with novelty. One man may begin it, but hundreds are carried with the tide. Some are invigorated by the experience, some are swept off their feet but recover, some pass on into real insanity. . . .

What might be called the school of D. H. Lawrence is clearly obsessed by the complex of sex, which the new psychology has advertised so widely. Such an obsession is not insanity, although it is often irrational and sometimes unbalanced. Yet what might come of it in later stages we have often wondered; and the "Ulysses" of James Joyce shows what may happen if the brakes are lifted and such an obsession allowed to run free.

Joyce is a man of distinct though peculiar genius, as his earlier "A Portrait of the Artist as a Young Man" proved. "Ulysses" demonstrates his genius in brilliant narrative passages of a candid realism almost unequalled in English. Mrs. Bloom, lying abed in meditation—a long chapter, without punctuation, of such incoherent but convincing reminiscence, as only Dickens, divinely drunk and inconceivably lewd, could have equalled—is a masterpiece, a dirty masterpiece, like certain Greek vases, yet still a *chef-d'œuvre*. But this is an episode, and, with other episodes of almost equal brilliance, makes up but a part of a vast book full of every extravagance of improvisation and experiment that a madhouse for the brilliantly insane could provide. If Bernard Shaw had gone crazy at thirty because of disappointed love, and if Max Beerbohm, George Moore, and Anatole France, each unbalanced by the repression of the sex instinct, had joined him in his cell, the four in collaboration might have produced such a book as "Ulysses"—but only, be it understood, if madness had deprived them of clarity and restraint. We do not wish to assert that, in our opinion, Mr. Joyce is mad. He is presumably sane or he would never have pushed through to completion such a monumental effort of scholarship and imagination as "Ulysses." But his book is mad. In spite of its brilliant episodes it is often obscure, as often incoherent, ordinarily extravagant, and sometimes vicious. Its indecency would have appalled Rabelais and frightened and disgusted Chaucer. Those vigorous geniuses were indecent where indecency served their purposes of mirth, satire, and the analysis of man. But "Ulysses" is indecent as the alcoholic is intoxicated, by uncontrollable necessity, driven by an obsession which will not let go. In spite of the originality of the attempt to present the history of one day in a group of minds in Dublin, such a book is valuable in a world trying to be sane, trying to save itself by humor or insight from the perversion of honest instincts and from mental confusion, only because of its new and brilliant technique, and its passages of undoubted genius.

We have had a good deal of nonsense uttered by the loud-voiced in criticism about "this transcendent work of genius," which, thanks to puritanic censorship, only the critic and a few of his friends have been able to read! Many, to whom Chaucer, Boccaccio, Rabelais, and "The Golden Ass" of Apuleius are not alien, hold a different opinion. A work of genius, with intervals of greatness, yes—but let us also assert the patent truth, through scores of pages a disgusting book, and, when the narrative clouds, wandering and confused. If we are, as one hopes, to have new, true, and frank treatment of sex as the central problem in life, let us beware, by this example, of what repressions too suddenly burst may do to the delicate mind of the artist.

A Specialist in Sex

SIGNS are not wanting, indeed they are abundant, that the most prepotent novelist of our day in the eyes of the younger writers of advanced fiction is D. H. Lawrence. As one of them has recently said, he fascinates them. That this should be so is interesting, and asks for an explanation. Lawrence is not popular as Kipling was, not magnetic like Stevenson, not venerable like Hardy. His spell is a subtler one than theirs; perhaps more dependent upon a change of mood which his work symbolizes and his readers recognize as a reflection of their own hearts.

Those who have been through "The Lost Girl," and "Aaron's Rod," will say that the index of Lawrence is sex, and that it is his sex interest which attracts youth by its boldness and its unrestraint.

If either audacity or novelty can get him followers, this may well be the answer. Mr. Lawrence has a new way with questions of sex. Sex for him is neither a subject to be avoided nor a topic not to be neglected in the development of his characters. It is the theme, the character, the story itself. He is obsessed by sex, and shows both the advantages and the disadvantages of an obsession.

As for the disadvantages, they are sometimes almost offensively obvious. With rare exceptions, Lawrence's characterizations turn upon the possession, or the lack, or the perversion, of the sex instinct. His men and women are consistently bedeviled by sex, and in his philosophizing so is he. For him, sex not merely interpenetrates the living world, which is true, but overshadows it, which is by no means often or necessarily true. One gets in reading the feeling one has had in certain societies of mystics, that every act, every word, every seeming irrelevant gesture, has its inner meaning, which in this instance is always phallic. Now our race may have often denied sex to their own hurt or ignorantly miscalled its manifestations by the names of hate, religion, irritability, courage, ambition, or wrath; but the age-long insistence of the wise upon keeping the sensual in its place and restraining passion by reason was not utterly void of sense, nor has human experience through the Christian ages gone for nought. Mr. Lawrence's intellectuals who long for frank paganism again, with freedom for the passions and a release of brute force, remind me of unrestful dowagers who advocate the Soviet or anarchy. There is still some virtue in the words of William Penn:

"Passion is a sort of Fever in the Mind, which ever leaves us weaker than it found us. It more than anything deprives us of the use of our judgment; for it raises a Dust very hard to see through. I have sometimes thought, that a Passionate Man is like a weak spring that cannot stand long lock'd. It is the difference between a Wise and a Weak Man; this

Judges by the Lump, that by Parts and their Connection."

Such, however, is by no means all the story. Lawrence is apparently afraid of the sex instinct. It is for him the urge of mother earth that no one can (and so should not) resist. And he pays to its superior powers a tribute of almost reverential study, which yields astonishing results. This is his advantage, and it is a great one. As the disciple knows his master, so Lawrence knows sex.

The great novels of sex of the nineteenth century were those of Thomas Hardy. By comparison, Lawrence's books are more subtle and more revealing. Hardy was interested in the results of the sex impulses as they display themselves in normal life. Sex wrecks Jude; sex ennobles and ruins Tess. Lawrence is not much interested in results. When sex is triumphant in Alvina, the lost girl, the story ends. *Her* story is just beginning, but the only aspect that interested Lawrence has concluded. Sex in itself and for itself is his fascination, and if this makes him narrow it also makes him shrewd.

Curiously enough, I find I must go back as far as Hawthorne for a satisfying parallel to D. H. Lawrence. Hawthorne also was obsessed by the inner workings of the human spirit. Hawthorne in "The Scarlet Letter" and "The Marble Faun" wrote profound studies of the metaphysics and psychology of sex. But it was sex in its relation to the moral nature of man which concerned the great neo-Puritan. The fate of mortal man was his inquiry, the result of the impact of soul in body upon soul in body for happiness and character and humanity. His work is on a larger scale, if not on a higher plane, than the novels of Lawrence. He is obsessed, but by no narrow obsession. He is a greater man, and his books are greater books. Nevertheless, Lawrence shares the advantages of the specialist. By concentrating on sex *per se,* by isolating it, in so far as it can be isolated, from the complex of human experience, by throwing the light of his mind upon that phase of the characters he chooses in which sex is dominant, he gets a scientific description, and an analytic perception not to be found in earlier work. He is a research novelist—a product of his day. And beside his studies of the sex nature of women the parallel work of the more brilliant Meredith seems haphazard.

Thus there is abundant reason why the younger generation here and in England, if they are especially interested in sex, should follow Lawrence with interest. And they *are* especially interested in sex: the abnormal life of wartime, the breakdown of many of the inhibitions of the pre-war period, the unrest that has followed moral disillusion, and the unsettlement of principles always associated with a period of change, all have emphasized sex, its urges and its problems, while the flood of light upon sex influences shed by the new psychology has, of course, contributed much.

But there is another prevailing reason for the spell which Lawrence seems to exercise over the more intellectual young. The favored characters in Mr. Lawrence's books—or, not to generalize too much, in "The Lost Girl" and "Aaron's Rod," which are the two books I have particularly in mind in this survey—betray unblushingly that "hard-boiled" egoism which is the War's aftermath and the time's response to philanthropy, liberalism, altruism, and such shibboleths of the nineteenth century. It is more than curious to list the novels of the last two years—particularly the first novels—of younger men and women, and to see how prevailingly egoism, self-development at all costs, ruthlessness, and the selfish generally are lauded by illustration and philosophically implied. "Not my will but Thine" is reversed in these books, and it is reversed in the books of D. H. Lawrence. Alvina, when sex flares within her, sneers at her environment and moves ruthlessly out of it, leaving wrecks behind her. She is incapable of love as we have used the term, and scornful of charity. Aaron, who flies from sex passion, hating it, as she flies towards it, dreading it, is even more selfful, more ruthless. I am not passing moral censure upon his desertions. That is not the point. It is their cold selfishness, a vigorous anti-Christian selfishness, asking for praise from the reader, that is the salient characteristic. Aaron's friends, Lilly excepted, are less strong than he, but even more selfish. Ciccio, in "The Lost Girl," is a pure pagan— I mean a Lawrentian pagan, who is moved solely by natural impulses conducing to the development and expression of self. The classic pagan, I fancy, would feel a little uncomfortable if he could read his modern definitions. Ciccio, one feels, would not even understand altruism. He would sniff at it and turn away, as a horse turns from cooked food, or a dog from jewelry. This uninhibited ego is the ambition of many in our times, and in Lawrence they find it frankly, discriminatingly apotheosized. If sex, epitomized and atomized, attracts the weaker to Lawrence's novels, it is his revolutionary egoism that stirs the stronger among his readers. But have his readers rightly understood their Lawrence?

If one is to believe the evidence of his two last novels, he is anything but a dilettante in sex psychology. Rather he is a philosopher-novelist offering means of escape from the torments of flesh. "The Lost Girl" is the story of Alvina Houghton, who escapes from small-town futility and the life of an old maid by yielding her body and its emotions utterly to a wandering Italian player, intellectually and temperamentally alien to her. The last very beautiful chapters of the book recount how her fastidious spirit is reconciled to the life of a peasant woman in the Italian mountains, not happy, but dumbly satisfied in her complete prostration before passion. "Aaron's Rod" recounts the adventures of a miner flying from the too exacting passion of his wife. Sex repels him, but having thrown off its urge he is restless until he learns that power or the submission to power may take its place. In the first book the woman yields to elemental passion and loses her intellectual life, but is saved from sterility;

in the second the man flies from passion, but must have a substitute.

It is not sex then, but the escape from its torments that Lawrence proposes to celebrate.

Let the urge be not the love mode but the urge of power, says Lilly in "Aaron's Rod," "then the great desire is not happiness, neither of the beloved nor of oneself. Happiness is only one of many states and it is horrible to think of fixing us down to one state. The urge of power does not seek for happiness any more than for any other state. It urges from within darkly, for the displacing of the old leaves, the inception of the new. It is powerful and self-central, not seeking its center outside, in some God or some beloved, but acting indomitably from within itself. And, of course, there must be one who urges, and one who is impelled. . . . The woman must now submit—but deeply, deeply, and richly. . . . Woman—and man too. Yield to the deep power-soul in the individual man, and obey implicitly. . . . Every man must fulfil his own soul, every woman must be herself, herself only. . . ." But, "we *must* either love or rule," and when love wears out, it will be rule, or obey.

Beautifully, as only a philosopher's novels can, do Lawrence's books illustrate this theory. Ciccio rules, and Alvina, in spite of her superior intellect, loves, submits, and profoundly obeys—leaves her own life and takes his, and is not happy, but satisfied, escaping the pangs of unsatisfied sex, though at what cost! For Aaron, the love mode is worn out. He will not submit to these women who love for their own purpose, who repulse the man when he is passionate and seek love satisfaction for themselves, and for itself. He will not submit to love, and unlike Ciccio he cannot make it submit to him. His wife demands, never yields. His mistress, the Marchesa, submits, but to the experience and not in any true sense to him. He is adrift, wasting his personality, aimless, afraid of the sex impulse in himself and in others. If he cannot love, cannot rule, says Lilly, then he must obey a man's will. He must find some power to serve; only so can he escape the tyranny of passion.

Well, this may be true, and only slavery or masterfulness may be able to save us from sex. Perhaps altruism, perhaps love, as we knew it, is bankrupt. Perhaps liberalism and the release of energies which it offered was a dream. Perhaps the ethics of Christianity were futile and are now obsolete. But it will take more than a powerfully saturnine novelist to convince us. Lawrence's liberals are singularly arid and futile, his Christians are mere pious platitudes. The only vigor in his books is a selfish vigor, the only intensity springs from sex. His example of a victim to the love urge is Jim, who wanders in a maudlin fashion wanting-to-be-loved by any and every one, and jumps on Lilly and pounds him in his wife's presence when he is told so. A singularly futile lot upon which to base a generalization. As an analysis of a shell-shocked society I find all this excellent. As a world philosophy it seems morbid moonshine, the reflections of frightened men running from passion to take shelter in power.

But it is not this philosophy which makes readers and admirers for Lawrence. It determines his estimate of humanity and guides his choice of characters for illustration. It makes his books unpleasantly dogmatic, and at the same time gives them the sincerity of work written out of faith and belief rather than mere observation. Yet whether his philosophy interests his readers is questionable. They are fascinated by results. Thanks to his obsession with sex he knows it as few men have known it, and probably for the first time in literature, certainly for the first time in English, he has got into fiction the true relationship between a neurotic woman and her husband, or her lover. Fear of sex drives him to a contemplation of power which can subdue and may displace it. And from thoughts of power he passes to studies in submission which calm his spirit, and produce in the fiction he makes of them a serene deliberation in which incidents and details have a new value and a transcending beauty. One cannot sufficiently praise the Italian chapters of "The Lost Girl." It is for this last, but still more because of his penetration into the secret places of sex, and for the egoism which springs from his philosophy and which medicines the restlessness which they also feel, that Lawrence (so I believe) is admired of his admirers.

As a stylist he is sometimes wonderful, but more often undistinguished. As a technician he is by no means perfect. As a mirror of his age, his glass is often bent and sometimes flawed. If, as some have said, he is the greatest writer of our period, it must be as Professor X is the greatest scientist of our times —in his own narrow field; or as Mr. Y is the greatest poet of our times—in free verse. Lawrence is the greatest novelist in our day—of the over- and the undersexed. That is an achievement, and I do not mean to sneer at it; but it marks him as thus far a special student of special circumstance, not as an artist of that breadth of seeing which the more temperate are willing to call great.

IV

Highbrow and Lowbrow

White Socks at the Symphony

AT a luncheon in New York recently the director of a great moving picture theater maintained that the art of the people was better conducted than art for the select. He said that he had attended a symphony concert where seventy performers in ill-fitting dress clothes played incomprehensible music against an ugly background of dirty gray, and that some of them very conspicuously under their black trousers wore white socks! For himself he preferred an orchestra in soft browns in a well-considered stage setting, playing Tchaikovsky between the reels to an accompaniment of appropriate colors and lights. He doubted the utility of an art the people could not understand, but what they did want he proposed to give them as perfect in every detail and circumstance as an obstinate idealism could make it.

The worm has turned and we could preach a volume from his text. It is certain that the makers of select and intellectual literature too often wear incongruous white socks with their pretentious costumes. Those exotic and expensive books with slovenly errors in the text; those magazines for particular people with illustrations so incongruous and contents so ill assorted and inharmonious that an editor of a baseball extra would blush for them; we know their kind. And we have pondered also over defects of taste and scholarship in snobbishly superior literature; over intellectual novels where the author has handled his plot like an amateur; over plays in verse where the dramatist forgets his audience and sometimes the stage. Intricate thoughts and an elevated artistic imagination are offered as excuse for dull or imperfect expression. But playing Ornstein does not permit a musician to play badly and to wear a red tie and white socks with his dress suit.

However, the chief moral is for popular, democratic literature, which may have to go to the movies for an education. To give the people what they like, but to give that perfectly, has not been a practice of American popular magazines. On the whole, they have written down to their audience, and so have the popular novelists, and neither has thought much of taste or art, or possessed them. There is very little evidence in their wares of the harmony—in magazines of picture, type, arrangement, color, and substance; in novels, of subject and style—which the great cinema theaters at least are seeking; and few signs of an attempted perfection at the level of popular sympathy. American popular magazines are ugly and they are hard to read. Their standards of taste and content have been stationary or have declined, while those of the moving picture houses have been going up.

Of course, the idea that what the public does not like or understand is "bunk," is "bunk" itself. The public is becoming rapidly educated (if you are an optimist) or becoming rapidly degraded (if you are a pessimist); but in any case a few of the public grow up daily and to them what was incomprehensible yesterday, like some music, becomes familiar and likable to-morrow. Tchaikovsky and the Russian ballet would have seemed "bunk" to the directors of twenty years ago. There is nothing to learn from this attitude; but when the leaders of the greatest of popular amusements begin to seek perfection it is time for editors and publishers to begin thinking. To lavish all the resources of art and intellect, and yet keep the interest of the democracy, that is a project with a future ahead of it. Perhaps it is a definition of the art of the democratic future out of which some greater art, more vital than anything we have at present, may arise. Perhaps it is merely good sense. Every one knows that where one man likes imagistic poetry a hundred prefer fox trots on the victrola, but that is no argument for giving up imagistic poetry. It is also no reason for continuing to write stale fox trots for scratchy victrolas. The victrola, the moving picture, and the popular magazine are the three great entertainers of the masses. They cannot be elevated too far without ceasing to be popular, but no such restriction limits their excellence.

Highbrow and Lowbrow

IN the thirteenth century a great advantage in knowing Latin was that if you cut a purse or slipped a knife between a fat monk's ribs you could claim "benefit of clergy" and be tried by an ecclesiastical court. In the eighteenth century a great advantage in knowing a little Greek was that it set you apart as a scholar and presumably a gentleman. In the twentieth century Greek and Latin have decayed, but the idea of caste which they fathered has remained to our hurt.

In the old days, critics, scholars, writers who were not mere space fillers, and the educated generally, felt that solidarity which arises from a common education. If snobbishly separated from the vulgar, they were at least fellows among themselves. They were all highbrows, whatever their profession; the lowbrows not only did not read Latin, they did not, in any real sense, read at all.

But the ancient order of highbrows is no longer united, and this is a pity. "Highbrow" we take to mean to-day a person professionally learned. All university professors, some ministers, and a few lawyers, doctors, and scientists are highbrows; those who possess and use learning without professing it are not. This is an absurd distinction. A metropolitan newspaper employs more expert knowledge in economics, history, and literature than many universities can boast. A novelist, essayist, or poet of the first rank must have behind him such an equipment of literature and social and esthetic history as might get him a university chair. As it happens, the universities have inherited the idea of an intellectual caste and make the most of it, to their own great hurt. If you are an intellectual you are either a professor or you are not, and if you are not, they ask, "What are you?"

Thus in our day there is less coöperation among real highbrows than ever before in the history of the world. If X, the critic, writes a brilliant essay upon Meredith and publishes it in a newspaper all the critics and many of the literary will read it, but it will probably remain unknown to "students" of Meredith, perhaps never be cited in their bibliographies. If Y, the "student" of Meredith, investigates his prose style and publishes in *Modern Language Notes*, slap will go his title on every card catalogue, every lady and gentleman, assiduously getting up Meredith for a dissertation or a monograph will read him—but by the learned in Meredith outside the universities he will probably never be read at all. Thus literary critics in the modern languages and professors of the same, make discoveries of new authors two years apart, and never know of the discrepancy. Thus critiques of poetry or of fiction run in two separate lines—one academic, one literary—and never meet or influence one another. Thus the two Americans who know most about the history of the drama may never know each other, and almost never hear of each other, because one is a college professor and rotates in an orbit of Modern Language meetings, class lectures, and special monographs, while the other publishes in popular newspapers and intellectual weeklies too radical for university consumption.

I say it is a pity. Professorial criticism and research need some blood and breath and purpose in them; professorial publication in the U. S. A. tends to the provincial, to much fussing in little areas. It lags behind our needs and disregards interest and worth. It is often dry and petty, like provincial conversation. And literature and criticism in America need more of the academic; need more bone to them, more background, more of that confident independence which comes from knowing what really happened in the past.

When is the compartment period of American culture going to end? When is the true distinction between highbrow and lowbrow, as between those who know and have taste and those who guess and have no taste, going to be recognized? The first step, it would seem, lies with the colleges. They must step out a little into the world and see what is happening there. The second step must come from the free intellectual. He must (horrid thought) be willing to take advice from those whose leisure has permitted a deeper study than his own. The *rapprochement* must come quickly, for the lowbrows are breeding by millions and already they control nine-tenths of the published word. They may sweep us all up together, professor, lecturer, journalist, critic, amateur, columnist, researcher, and aspiring editor, and let us flutter like a Sunday newspaper into the waste baskets of futility.

Curious and True

THE professions of letters and of journalism have always lived by laws and customs of their own. Poverty and respectability, for example, have been often associated instead of antithetic as in the greater world; men have been valued for their promise even more than for their achievements; and parsnips have been buttered by fine words with satisfaction all round. The most remarkable of all these incongruities is to be found in modern New York. Much has been heard of the radical, critical, intellectual iconoclast, and more has been heard from him in scathing ridicule of the popular, conventional, time-serving editor. In New York they are usually not two people but one! Right hand is criticizing left; right brain lobe is damning left brain lobe of a double personality.

The explanation is simple. Popular magazines which serve millions and metropolitan newspapers printed by hundreds of thousands have become industries of magnitude employing thousands of specialists in typewriter and pen. But writing, even hurried writing, is an affair of the intellect; brains awake and in complete control are required for it; and the same is true of editing, even in its humblest departments. Reading also is required, vigorous reading of wide extent that feeds the mind, extends the vocabulary, and sends new ideas sparking. Hence the men and women drawn into the great editorial machine of New York are sure to be "intellectuals," have probably fed upon the strong meat of provocative books, and—far more than their fellow Americans—are likely to be scornful of the merely popular, the certainly pleasant, and the agreeably superficial, which is a fair description of much in contemporary American literature.

They staff the periodicals of vast circulation; they solicit and edit material; they execute, if they do not always originate, policies calculated to win popular success. The more "lowbrow" the periodical the more "highbrow" its editors is true enough to be a useful aphorism in New York.

This is very amusing. It is amusing to consider that "Lady Betty," who writes a column on cosmetics, probably wears horn spectacles and paints scenery for the Provincetown Players. It is titillating to learn that the associate editor of *Frivolous Fiction* is a poet so serious that only Ezra Pound can follow him. It is devastating to be told that the demon detective story writer of the *Dispatch's* Sunday supplement practices psychoanalysis in the evenings and has been acquitted of a charge of obscenity on the ground that his novel (to which he signed his real name) was too literary to be dangerous. But the final emotion is not amusement.

For one wonders whether some of the insincerity in popular editing which is so marked now and so highly objectionable to people of honest tastes is not

due to the double personality of so many editors.
Those affectionate editorials that have so evidently
had intimacy injected as the drug clerk squirts syrup
into malted milk; those murmuring preludes in italics
which discourse lyrically of forthcoming stories; those
familiar "old hoss" and "old dear" blurbs upon the
merit of the magazine; all such insincere writing is designed to trick the public into thinking that the editor
loves them, and is the product of clever minds profoundly skeptical of the value of what they have to sell,
but quite aware of why and how it is salable. Look
elsewhere for the same sort of thing and you will find
it in the sister art of advertising, where the same situation exists; for years a selection of the best minds of
a literary cast has gone pell-mell from college into advertising, as a profession that offered opportunity to
those competent in words, and a surer income than literature.

We are not concerned at this writing with the economic causes of these strange circumstances, or their
cure, if any exists short of strangulation. But the effect
on popular literature does concern us, for it is not
good. With one hand the intellectual provides literature for the mass and with the other throws stones and
contumely at what he has produced. That is neither
honest, nor the road to good editing. A clever pen
may hide insincerity; but it is revealed in the choice
of stories that, with a certain contempt, hit below the
popular taste instead of above it, and in magazines
that are blatant without real emotion and vulgar with-

out excuse. And we who love good reading suffer from self-opinionated smartness, and the public, which asks not for cake, perhaps, but still for honest bread and butter, is given adulteration and machine-made biscuit with pink icing on the top.

I propose a Great Experiment. Let the esoteric despisers of the popular who at present wield mush spoons for the great Republic resign and go into the soup, soap, or shoe business (not, however, the advertising end!), leaving the public's reading to be chosen by those who love literature enough to care for its simpler manifestations. Or, since skill in editing is not a common gift, and we cannot recruit our departments from sympathetic barkeepers and humane hotel clerks, let them not resign, or not all of them, but broaden their minds and open their hearts. It is possible (and advisable) to be both editor and intellectual, but it is impossible to be both sentimental editor and supercilious intellectual at one and the same time without offense to the right thinking and ultimate sterility.

Easy Come, Easy Go

THE great modern educator is the advertising man. He has sold the advertising idea to the producers of everything, from patent bread to new religions, and they must have space and ever more space to talk about their wares. Magazines multiply, newspapers double and quadruple in size, and an infinity of sheets, half sheets, columns, and corners must be filled with stories, facts, news, opinions. For all this there must be readers, and so every resource of persuasion, argument, admonition, and seduction is practised to make easy-going Americans buy and consume a mass of writing that would have staggered Rome and buried Greece.

The more advertising, the more general literature we must be made to read. It is a new kind of compulsory education, but the object is not to educate or even to amuse us, but rather to make us believe that we need to be amused or educated. When we are told that we must know about the World Court or how to hold our forks, what is meant is that unless we buy newspapers or magazines no one will advertise in them. If advertising should cease upon a midnight, the morning after would be the first day of revelations. The news would go into four sheets instead of fourteen, and magazines would print twenty thousand copies instead of two hundred thousand. It would soon be made clear that at least ten thousand short stories would not have to be written, that an equal number of special articles telling us all about everything was dispensable, and that if the number of eggs laid by prize hens, the attitude of the Southwest toward Prohibition, or the recent history of Poland had to be known, we could dig out the facts ourselves. The saw would cease to whine in the spruce forests, the news-stand would shrink to an apple cart, and rest at last would come to reading America.

This forced draught education for the sake of the advertiser is by no means without its value. We Americans are the best-informed people in the world. We know a little about everything. There was a howl from their elders some years ago when it was discovered that school children and college students had too little general information, did not know who Clemenceau was, or whether Siam was north or south of China. Of course, the truth was that they had not yet come under the influence of the new education. They were not made to read magazines and newspapers, for having little money to spend they did not interest advertisers. They were being taught, by the old education, quite a little about a few things, instead of learning, like their parents, a very little about many things. But that difficulty was promptly overcome by giving them courses in magazine information, so that the glib practice of seeing the world by paragraphs soon became a habit.

Now, doubtless, the spread of general information makes us more intelligent, but does it make us any wiser? What is a fact worth without its context? What is a conclusion worth if we do not read the argument? How far does the description of a book serve, if we never read the book? They did things somewhat differently in the later Roman Empire, when, as civilization grew sluggish, libraries shrank to volumes of excerpts, and education consisted of studying the easy parts of hard books. We are expanding instead of contracting, have much more writing instead of less; but if most reading is to be by excerpt, and most education to consist of knowing the easy parts of many kinds of learning, are things so very different after all?

Europe views with amazement the violent tides of American opinion. In 1918 most were for the League of Nations, whatever that might mean; in 1920 most were against foreign entanglements, whatever that might mean. Was there information available? Tons of it? Did we read it? By millions of paragraphs mixed in with anecdotes, recipes, statistics, short stories, and scandalous biographies. And so with prohibition, and feminism, and sex, and the new psychology, and the Ku Klux Klan.

Easy come and easy go describes this kind of reading and this kind of education. Our brains are like clenched fingers. If we grasp anything more we must drop something first. But if the advertising profession innocently and for the best commercial reasons has brought the practice to its present flourishing condition, it did not begin it. The active American intelligence has always desired to know a little more about everything, especially if the knowledge came easily. This was played upon. We sought a democratic road to learning, and thought that we had found it.

Getting Unstandardized

JOURNALISM apparently is chasing the Ford car and will soon catch up with its dust. Newspapers are being standardized into systems of interchangeable parts with alarming rapidity. Every consolidation of great journals automatically results in a feeding of more minds by fewer hands. As syndication broadcasts further and further, the local newspapers become more and more replicas each of its neighbor. You can follow a famous cartoonist across the continent by buying a paper in every town of over fifty thousand inhabitants; and two or three poetasters and platitudinists supply daily wit and wisdom for millions. Soon the only remaining differences between the *Wistaria Herald* and the *Chebunkport News* must be searched for in the local events columns, the society news, and the obituary record. Everything else, including the editorials, will be syndicated.

It looks like a chill time ahead for native talent. The local journalist, no matter how remote, must compete at the very beginning with standardized products from New York. Well, that is what has happened to the local manufacturer, the local butcher, the neighborhood druggist, to individual industries generally. It is part of the industrial revolution which only the ignorant supposed would let journalism and literature go their ways unaffected. We can deplore many of the results, while noting that the level of rural journalism has been raised. But originality, individualism, self-reliance in the community have been frosted.

Protesting against inevitable change—the daily occupation of many honest men and women—is a dismal pastime leading nowhere. Newspapers will be increasingly standardized, and in heart, brain, and function generally more and more Americans will become standardized also. Nothing but a disaster like Russia's can prevent the leveling up which is part of our idea of democracy.

Yet while Americans by millions are getting standardized as soon as they can afford it, other Americans by thousands are getting unstandardized as rapidly as they know how. It is just as much the age of breaking away from stale conventions, the age of new individuality, as it is the age of mass thinking. The admirers of originality, the appreciators of the fine, the purchasers of the excellent and rare, increase marvelously. Magazines succeed that could not have lived a year two decades ago; periodicals of vast circulation print contributions that in the old unstandardized days would have been thought fit for a few connoisseurs only; the Theater Guild grows fat upon highly unconventional plays; even literary criticism shows signs of a faint popularity.

To put it flatly: the vast majority in this country is possessed by the devil of uniformity, and pursues its own vanguard, driving down hill like the Gadarene swine to the destruction of individuality. Not the packing trust, not Henry Ford, not the Rockefeller and Carnegie institutions, not all the organization of all the institutions in the world can stop them, although education may make the steep road safer. But, in violent reaction, if you please, or because the time had come, or from some ineradicable need of human nature, at this moment the refusal to become a mere numeral dressed in nationally advertised clothing has become positive. The minority is usually as worth watching as the majority, even when it is a minute minority. And it is conceivable that the great leveling up which began in this country and is now its chief characteristic, is a plowing and harrowing and grading of soil where the new seed may grow. This is the optimist's view. In any case, let us watch with more sympathy our freaks, cranks, experimenters, self-expressionists, rebels, bohemians; our re-reformers, Tories, knockers, literary gadflies; our men who try to live by principle as well as accommodation, and women who refuse to be dominated by fabricated convention. Standardizing is a useful economic process, but if it sweeps beyond method and mechanism, personal worth and personal happiness are both threatened. Real achievement becomes more difficult and less appreciated. Personality fades. The world becomes duller because life begins to plod like a machine. Only rebellious reaction can save us.

Who Speaks for the People?

ROLLERS of easy critical phrases are always talking about great literature and how it expresses a race or a nation. The truth of the matter is that great literature expresses first of all the man that writes it, and is just as likely to give utterance to what a nation isn't as what it is. We talk of the austere Hebraicism of the Old Testament as if Jeremiah had spoken for the Hebrew race instead of against it. His particular sample of great literature was about as representative of the vain and foolish nation he chastised as a Methodist prohibitionist's of a "wet" community. Did Florence speak through the Dante she drove into exile? Is Cervantes the voice of Spain? The great writers are often protesters, minority leaders, crying sometimes, like Milton, in a wilderness of lost ideals.

The United States has suffered, like every other country, by the hand of the generalizer. Foreigners who assume that our best literature best represents us are often misled. They see what they call a "dollar civilization" and read an idealistic literature. Assuming that the two are necessarily parts of a harmonious whole, they invent a strange creature which they call the American, and then are puzzled because we do not act as if we were made in his image.

The truth is that the main currents of American

life have almost always flowed quite away from our best literature, and sometimes the two are as divergent as crossroads on a plain. The gentle aristocracy of Irving belongs in a period when levelers were breaking up the very idea of a republic of classes. Cooper, himself a democrat, writes stories of primitive feudal romance which persuade Europe that what had become a trading nation was the scene of the last stand of chivalry and adventure for its own sake. At the height of the great rush across the Appalachians and over the prairies, when the mind of the nation seemed given over to land speculation and bitter struggles to subdue to profit a thousand miles of virgin soil, Emerson writes of unworldliness and Thoreau retires to Walden to live as nearly as may be with no possessions at all. When the first beauty of Colonial America was giving way to business blocks and unproportioned houses, when a taste inherited from the decorous eighteenth century was being debauched by haste and lack of tradition, Poe sang the cult of pure beauty and rivaled in esthetic detachment the best of the Old World. While the austere moral code of the Puritans was being formalized and prettified in a thousand small towns of the new West, where rules took the place of spiritual ardors, Hawthorne raised the moral imagination to heights not equaled since. After the Civil War, in the most debased period of our history, given over to ruthless exploitation of a continent and sordid competition for individual wealth, Walt Whitman hymns complete democracy for masses who cannot understand him; Mark Twain jokes, and satirizes the most humorless generation we have known.

And to-day, with a vibrative energy that Europeans comment upon with amazement, an energy that presses like a coiled spring upon material development, what is our most characteristic literature? Not epics of expansion, not romances of virile activity (we have them, but they are not literature), but works of satire, of criticism, of pessimistic self-analysis, books which protest against, or make fun of, or deny the apparent attributes of American civilization. Instead of a Marlowe, a Fielding, a Dickens, a Hugo, we have Sinclair Lewis, Mrs. Wharton, Hergesheimer, Cabell, Zona Gale, Sherwood Anderson, Mencken, and Scott Fitzgerald.

Of course, there is nothing surprising in all this, except to those who live by generalizations. Good literature, like good taste, the Christian virtues, and manners, is usually the function of a minority. If instead of Emerson, Thoreau, and Hawthorne the pioneers and real estate speculators had made our literature in the '40s, the results would have been deplorable. And if, to state the case more fairly, material expansion instead of transcendentalism had been the inspiration of that literature, we should have little to be thankful for. But the majority has rights and presents opportunities. That the United States at the very peak of its power and activity should breed chiefly critics is surprising and perhaps unfortunate. There is a fine chance for a poet who, like Tennyson, in the England of his day, is positive and dynamic, instead of negative or analytical. There is a gorgeous opportunity for novels of epic breadth which, like Hugo's and Scott's and, in a little different sense, Tolstoy's, go with the instinct of the populace instead of against it. The fineness of America has long since and again and again gone into books. Its bigness has eluded us.

If You Must Resolve

HENRY ADAMS describes the American traders in the early days as being so shrewd and so intelligent that the English thought they were all rascals. It was the day of the wooden nutmeg and of the clipper rig. There is no doubt that we Americans then had a reputation for versatility, that our minds, and especially Yankee minds, were flexible, so that we were handy at anything. There were no specialists in the United States; every one could do everything. If a farmer began to preach, or a blacksmith went into politics, or a pencil maker set up as philosopher, or a shopkeeper became a general, that was not surprising. And everything was every one's business. The country store debated theology with as little hesitation as it discussed eggs; Benjamin Franklin went into electricity and printing with equal zest; there were New Englanders who ran through almost every trade and profession in a single lifetime.

Whether we have lost our versatility is disputed, but we are certainly losing our flexibility of mind. The country is getting stiff-necked and single-tracked. It is crystallizing into castes. There is the caste of esthetic intellectuals whose minds are set like a telescope on things fine, difficult, and remote. If opinion is not subtle for them it does not exist, and they have almost lost the power of simple, obvious speech. There is the caste of business men, who see everything in terms of production and trade. If religion or science or politics is to be talked to them it must be in their own language. Indeed, many skilful magazines have made rapid progress by reducing all knowledge and aspiration to a business basis. The American business man is becoming just such an intolerable highbrow as the soldier was in Shakespeare's day and the priest a little later. He refuses to step outside of his shop and you must talk to him in his vocabulary or not at all. All honor to the notable exceptions to this unfortunate rule. There is the caste of those devoted to the uplift, for whom a whole literature is published, and who will not go outside of it. These are the easily shocked and the readily intolerant. But their stiffness is in words more than deeds. They represent a very honest American inheritance and they have kept the American adaptability in practice. Put them in a new town, or in politics, or where business is business, and their hearts are better than their heads, and their deeds much more elastic than their opinions. It is words that upset them—words that smack too much of levity, or that name harsh facts of life. Here they are stiff as clay.

And there is the highbrow, in the sense usually given to that useful but badly used word. The caste of pedants has some excuse in a country where so many people balk at words of more than four syllables, and believe that any affair, such as religion, philosophy, or science, outside their front yard, is too erudite for them. But the pedant who insists upon discussing everything in the abstract and chooses his words with a view to impressing the ignorant is as much of an obstacle to free moving interests as the lowbrow who will care for nothing not related to trade, food, love, or sport. The highbrow becomes dangerous, however, only when he forms a caste and lives within it. That is the condition of many scientists to-day who talk, write, and work for each other, using a jargon of their own, and regarding the world outside much as the Greeks viewed the barbarian. This is one reason why thousands of apparently intelligent people can deny the fact of evolution without knowing what the word means, and run counter to the most elementary instructions of modern science in their governments and their lives.

If we are to make a resolution, let it be for flexible minds, especially in our reading. It would be a good experiment to try a book or a magazine different in subject and in kind from past experience. If builders would read "The Stones of Venice" and brokers try Sophocles; if professors would experiment with *The Saturday Evening Post* and ministers read Anatole France; if everyday people would be as willing to read books (not digested articles) upon the new physics and psychology, upon decoration, geology, Asiatic religion, or the history of romanticism as our ancestors were ready to be jack at any trade, what a brisking and furbishing of the general curiosity would result! And what a boon it would be for writers, who might dare to be human without fear of being called cheap, or thoughtful without expecting some one to shout "highbrow!" The mind that begins to spin itself in like a caterpillar into a cocoon is dying, no matter how perfectly it functions within its self-made walls. The mental health of man can best be judged by his horizons.

Aristocracy

YES—it is time. Democracy in literature has had its swing with scarcely a resistant tremor, and now a reaction is overdue. The common man, once part of the mob or chorus, has become a theme; the commonplace man who fails consistently or succeeds ignobly is the hero of serious novels and problem plays; style has become prosaic, poetry by choice deals with the familiar, romance sheds its glow over the exploits of democratic pioneers or gilds the tale of how very ordinary people make unnecessary millions. When Defoe, Dryden, Addison, Steele taught how to smooth rhythmic English into good, practical prose the movement was beginning, and now it culminates in a vast expressiveness of the commonplace in which the mediocre at last have justice done them and the vulgar dominate at will.

The democratic impulse is vigorous, the aristocratic impulse has been weak. Aristocratic literature in our day, and particularly in America, has been merely snobbish, or freakish, or it has dealt with whims or subtleties, or been made in nervousness or eroticism. It has been weakly intellectual, piling up the obscure and the difficult like obstacles in a road. In the novel it has been fiercely but hopelessly satiric of the ugly and the mean. The aristocrat has been marked not by what he could do, but by what he did not like.

The popular mind refuses a negative conception and so has had to satisfy the eternal craving for an ideal by creating an aristocracy for itself. The popular aristocrat of democratic literature has been a caricature. If a woman, her superiority lies in clothes, perfumes, and a command of servants and lovers. If a man, ease in spending and a so-called "New York manner" (borrowed from the advertisements) seem to be the attributes. The democrats in recent literature are often good types worthy of a place in the Elysian Fields of literature. The aristocrats are parvenus, more vulgar than the common people, shadows or travesties at best. In its failure to create its like, the aristocratic spirit proves that it has been weak.

Our society since the Renaissance has been a history of the slow uplifting of the masses. The curve of democracy has been upward and will continue upward as long as the common man from generation to generation gains in education and in economic power. But if this is a reason for the decline of leadership and the submergence of the fine in the fair, it is no excuse. The principle of deference to the superior mind is not lost in democratic development, it is merely obscured or released as the public grows confident in its success or is chastened by its failures. An enlightened democracy (it is a platitude to say it) will cherish its intellectual aristocrats and dislike the cheap Jacks and Jills who represent privilege without excellence. I do not argue that democracy is enlightened, or soon will be; yet, since excess invariably brings its opposite we may hopefully expect a reaction.

Democratic literature has been speeding up the wrong street and landed on the dumps. Fineness of spirit, the willingness to do without rather than do badly, the preference for quality over quantity, pride in achievement rather than pride in recognition, hate for the cheap, the easy, the vulgar, and mean, good humor that comes from liberality, wit that explodes grossness—all these important parts of real aristocracy have been scattered on the way, and now the engine runs filthily amid the empties and hand-me-downs of a slovenly generation.

Some fine morning our American will look at his face in the mirror of a new book and say: I am getting tawdry; I am small-minded; I am vulgar. Who will save me from a condition already uncomfortable and likely to be unfashionable! And, then, if there are real aristocrats who can write, their moment will have come. But their task will not be easy. They will have to popularize such unpopular things as leisure and obstinacy and skepticism and responsibility. They will have to attack current conceptions of happiness and success. They will have to defend the past without illusion and describe the present without sentimentality. They must know how both to love and to hate.

V

Studies

Mark Twain

THE line of familiar titles in an edition of Mark Twain to the inquiring eye seems stretched upon a curve, which rises into humorous extravagance and dips into ironic seriousness or passionate indignation as memory passes from "Roughing It" and "Innocents Abroad" through "Joan of Arc" and "The Mysterious Stranger." The lift and fall of the curve is recurrent from the beginning to the end. It represents an essential quality of our prime humorist's art of which more needs to be said.

Mr. Van Wyck Brooks in his excellent study of Mark Twain has noticed this vagary of his genius, loud exaggerations followed by sudden pitches downward into cynicism and irony. He finds therein a symptom of the tragedy of an American genius cribb'd, cabined, and confined by his environment. Mark, the coarse, free soul of Mark, was suppressed by respectability and a prim wife. He who knew what life was like on the raw edges of a continent was checked on every side by bourgeois conventions. He must not offend good taste in his writing, as he did once a day at least in his speech; he must not speak of sex; he must not attack God, or morality, or the government. He must write what would sell. And as every one of these prohibitions sat upon his turbulent spirit like an ill-fitting saddle upon a broncho, he was thwarted in his attempt to express life as he knew it, and gave signs of his distress in nervous overemphasis, a guffawing humor, and sudden plunges into a pessimism as extravagant as his buffooneries.

I am not quoting Mr. Brooks. I am merely summing up what in general I understand to be his diagnosis of the intellectual disease which kept Mark Twain from his best development and was responsible for his sudden rushes between extremes. Probably he is right enough as criticism goes, unless, like some psychologists, he wishes to explain everything by complexes. Most artists are suppressed in one way or another, and not only in America. Yet it is arguable, nevertheless, that Clemens was the kind of spirit that needed a certain amount of suppression, without which he would have fizzed his life through like an uncapped soda spring. And there are some native American sources for this Clementian method of hurling the reader into pessimism from the midst of a laugh which should be mentioned before we begin to talk of bourgeois wives and an unsympathetic public.

Before Mr. Brooks wrote it was the fashion to explain the explosive exaggerations which offend the delicate in Mark Twain's books, by saying that exaggeration was the humor of the frontier, just as it was the humor of primitive epics of primitive people. Mark Twain got it there; Bret Harte got it there—you find it in the movies and Western stories to-day. I do not accept this explanation as sufficient. Frontier humor is a literary convention, like the comic darky or the stage Englishman. The contemporary frontiersman is a quiet, rather serious fellow. Of course, his experiences are likely to be in the large, and when he gets back he boasts—and literature begins to be made. Yet boasting was never Mark Twain's way, which was to use exaggeration for stamping, beating, hammering in, not an exploit, but an idea. He might have learned boasting on the frontier, but he learned his technique of humor elsewhere. It came from the lecture platform.

The popular lecture of Mark Twain's youth was not the sonorous address of an Emerson or the informative travelogue of our own day; it was a funny lecture, laugh provoking, touching upon the pathetic, but in the main ridiculous. Artemus Ward (see how he gave his benediction to Mark in Carson City), Petroleum V. Nasby, later Bill Nye, were its headliners. It was a lecture in which every laugh was calculated, fished for as in musical comedy. Nothing subtle could get over; there must be great exploding jokes, which were funny when they were said and twice as funny as they reverberated in the mass mind. "The report of my death is greatly exaggerated." That was the kind which made "faces seem to split from ear to ear and canes perform like pile-drivers."

Mark Twain, a failure at prospecting, a failure at casual newspaper work, broke in San Francisco after his Honolulu trip, and on the way to down and out entered the lecture field as a last hope, remembering his success as Governor of the burlesque Third House in Carson City. He entered as a laugh-maker, as a potential rival of Artemus Ward, whom he had long admired. He never left it. A quite unexpected success with his first audience committed him to the platform. For the next few years he was a lecturer by profession. It is a question whether he did not always regard himself as a lecturer by profession. Certainly that was what he fell back upon in the hard times that smote him at the height of his prosperity. He adopted wholesale, as any one may test for himself, the conventions of the humorous lecture—its anecdotes, its exaggerations, its overemphasis particularly.

The style of the humorous lecture is in all his prose. The sudden, incongruous transitions from serious to comic, the paradoxes, the careful preparation for a point, the rubbing in of an idea, the mock boasting, the exaggeration which carries absurdity to the bursting point, are all there and so derived. One half at least of the qualities of his style which make it seem rude, unfinished, unbalanced, boisterous, and also exuberant and alive are due to no inward psychology of the man whatever (except his liking for this sort of thing), but just to the simple fact that Mark, when he wrote, saw the lips of an audience quivering before him.

I distrust also the too easy conclusion that Mark Twain's almost feverish pessimism was a result of suppression; that the true Mark Twain, who had seen raw things and wanted to tell them, escaped now and then, baffled and angry, from the control of Samuel Clemens, the respectable American, and his very respectable wife. Mark Twain's training in good manners undoubtedly soured his temper, but it was never Mrs. Clemens that made him a pessimist. We forget that Clemens was a humanitarian with a frontier experience.

Clemens, as a youth, shared the experiences which in our modern romance of the frontier we neglect. The communities in which he lived were little acquainted with security. Fortunes moved up and down with frightful rapidity. If misery was rare, the constant illusion of speedy wealth was common, and disappointment was doubled by the magnitude of expectation. Every one except Indians, half-breeds, negroes, and the poorest of poor whites had almost been, or might yet be, wealthy. There were always Tennessee lands, or untried claims, or new allotments that might, and sometimes did, soar into riches. It was a gambler's world, with rapid fluctuations the rule, not the exception. Only drifters, floating westward to some new prospect and content to do without settled comfort, had a status which remained unchanged and the security of a future pretty much like the past.

And the cards were stacked in this gambling world of the frontier, stacked against the negro and Indian; stacked also against the real pioneers, the men who discovered and located, who broke ground and took the risk. It was the greedy ones who followed that picked up the prizes their weary hands had dropped.

A strange environment brought misfortunes upon the hard working and the innocent. And these men, as I have said, tasted success in dreams such as they would never have hoped for in the safety of back East. When they failed, therefore, they failed heavily. It was not the loss of a few soggy acres or a vein of quartz; it was wealth and estate that went a-glimmering. Mark Twain's adventures as a prospector are amusing as he tells them in retrospect in "Roughing It," but they were almost tragic as he lived them.

He was in fact conversant with the ups and downs of frontier fortune as were few minds as sensitive as his. He was a gambler himself in the frontier sense, always dreaming largely and usually disappointed; always trying his luck in the attempt to achieve security; and when he failed as he did, also largely, the lesson of his youth was emphasized; life itself is insecure and often unjust. That platform boisterousness of his has covered much of what he was thinking on the Mississippi, in Carson City, and in San Francisco. It came out later, the richer for maturity and experience.

In effect, Mark's high spirits were a corollary to his tendency towards profound depression. Born cynics seldom have high spirits, because they are pessimists by temperament. But there was nothing temperamental in Twain's pessimism. He could be cheered as readily as depressed. It was the way that life as he had experienced it increasingly made him feel; and when he felt he felt so strongly that any wild humor was preferable that would keep him off. A humanitarian with thin skin and a sense of humor is likely to suffer more than most men for the interest he takes in life. Reread the feud scene in "Huckleberry Finn" and you will agree that such a man had to joke. If he had been Russian he would have written in a tragic key and then drunk himself to death. Better to have let off steam in buffoonery and have remained inconsistent, American, and Mark Twain.

Indeed, far from suppressing him, respectable life, where virtue and hard work got its reward, set Twain free. He was not meant for pioneering. Security, so far as I can see, was his goal from the beginning. As a gambler he was a bad guesser, usually in hard luck. Interstate traffic on the Mississippi in '61 became the least secure of professions; he got on the wrong side first in the Civil War; prospecting was not his forte; lecturing was too slow—he tried to push on faster by publishing and was driven back to the platform. From the beginning he is seeking an income, a wife, a house in Hartford, leisure to write; and again and again the old frontier fortune he had brought along trips him. Security, he felt, ought to be obtainable by one who in his youth had never known it, and so he seeks it more and more angrily as the way is blocked or twisted. He knew much better than the children of settled communities the varieties of fortune that wait upon life. Being humanitarian he added other men's experience to his own, living, like many Americans, very much in the minds of his friends; and the prospect of it all made him a pessimist; not a philosophical pessimist; there is no reasoned philosophy in Clemens; but a humane pessimist rebelling against human experience that perforce made him either laugh or weep.

If sophisticated critics have difficulty in comprehending the vagaries of Mark Twain's humor it is because they rely too much upon his psychology and not enough upon the circumstances of his life. They do not understand his boisterousness because it is not a literary boisterousness, nor his pessimism because it is not a literary pessimism, the first being a lecture habit by which he roused his own mind to humorous pitch and set his audience laughing, the second a direct expression of brooding thought which uses words in default of action. Twain was never a man of letters, in the sense that such a writer imposes his emotion upon words. With him it was a question of stirring an audience by the handiest means, or if his mood was serious, speaking out to relieve his heart. When he produced great literature it was an accident of his genius, and in this row of volumes there is not much of it. If he had not obtained some security he might have just lectured all his life; if his experience had not been so rich he would have written nothing to endure.

It is felt that Clemens would have accomplished more if he had lived elsewhere than in a crude and guffawing America. The New Englanders of his day thought, of course, that he had been ruined for literature by living in the West. I deny both propositions.

There is no reason to suppose that if his later environment had been less respectable he would have gone deeper into human nature and omitted less, especially with reference to sex. Sex did not interest him one half so much as other human problems, religion, for example, and in this he was true to the type of his ablest contemporaries. The famous naughty letters which Howells could bring himself neither to read nor to destroy prove nothing except that Twain could be naughty when he chose. To have been facetious in sex as he was facetious elsewhere would certainly not have increased his fame, and there is every indication in his books that amorous adventure as a main theme of life did not interest him.

If he had spent his youth in New England or Old England he might have escaped the lecture platform at a vicious moment. That must be admitted. He might have gone in for writing first instead of talking and developed a tasteful genius instead of a merely powerful one. But then he would never have known frontier America, would have found security young, or never missed it, would have been funny in some different fashion and never ragingly pessimistic at all. In fact, the peculiar combination of elements which sometimes mars, but also makes, Mark Twain would have never existed, and we should have missed "Huckleberry Finn," "Tom Sawyer," "Life on the Mississippi," and "The Man That Corrupted Hadleyburg." Poe might have lived in Paris or London; but not Samuel Clemens, if he was ever to become Mark Twain.

A Poet Scientist

MANY have written of Hudson as a passionate yet unsentimental lover of nature, and as a stylist of as much distinction as charm. It is not because I am neglectful of these qualities that I choose to discuss his reputation as a modern classic from another angle, but rather because his growing reputation provokes a desire to place him in contemporary literature by some description less general than "stylist" and by some attribution more specific than "nature writer." He is, in fact, a lonely but important rebel in the revolt against the evils of industrialism, a revolt which will one day be seen to be a distinguishing characteristic of some of the finest writing of our time. Pampas rover, bird lover, tramper of the downs, he stood apart, fought in his own way, was a leader whom few followed, and a writer whom few read. Now that he is both dead and famous, his secret begins to be patent.

A hundred years of science and invention have committed us to industrialism. We shall never go back to the self-contained condition of the primitive state; we shall never give up machinery. Butler's dream of a revolutionary renunciation of mechanical aid, lest machinery should master men, is a dream only. Nothing less than a vast calamity breaking down civilization utterly could change the course of our development toward a greater and greater reliance upon labor-saving devices, and the resultant concentration in cities and standardization of the means of livelihood, amusement, and war.

A brilliant and truculent group of critics, of whom G. K. Chesterton in England and Ralph Adams Cram in this country are leaders, have attacked this flat ugliness of industrialism with parallels drawn from history as they read it. They wish us to go back to the Middle Ages, where man, so they say, was still instinctively artistic, where he loved what he worked upon, believed in more than his dinner, and if less comfortable in body was healthier in spirit and happier in soul. It is questionable, however, whether the twelfth and thirteenth centuries, as they reconstruct them, are much more historical than Erewhon and Utopia. Seen through a cathedral window or read in the laws of a guild, the past looks attractive. So will twentieth century America, studied in the memorials of Bronxville, Berkeley, or Bryn Mawr. In any case we will not and cannot go back.

There is even less to go upon in the esthete's protest against modernism. He sees the tide of mediocrity washing higher and higher over education, art, magazines, newspapers, most of all over daily life itself, and, not liking the game, refuses to play in it. He takes refuge in sheer egotism, escaping from reality to the exotic or the abnormal, both in what he likes and what he does. It is the impulse which took men and women to the monasteries and convents in the

Middle Ages, but it is far less catholic. The esthete's retreat from the noisy world of Fords, linotypes, subways, and general education is a hole-in-the-wall, large enough for himself only.

These protestants against the way we moderns live are rocks in the stream, but Hudson was a part of the stream himself. He was, as I understand him, as much a product of the age of observation as the gas engine or the research chemist. Although his books are literature, his motive power was science. He was as curious as a Greek, but with that desire to specialize in a given field—with him plant and animal life—which is so thoroughly modern. He is an intellectual brother of Darwin, Stephenson, Franklin, Humboldt, and Huxley. But those closest to him are Fabre, with his backyard universe of insects, Thoreau of Walden, Audubon, John Muir, and Agassiz, who was

> Patient to spy a sullen egg for weeks,
> The enigma of creation to surprise.

He belongs with these men, and especially with Muir, because while science was his stimulus and the factor which made him diverge from other masters of English prose in his time, he remained to old age in that first mood of the nineteenth century, which was as poetic as it was scientific. The popular science writers of to-day who discourse of the wonders of the universe and try to romanticize the triumphs of science are weak by comparison with these patriarchs of our age. Either, like H. G. Wells, they use science as a means

to a quite unscientific message, or they merely describe
or explain. They take their material at second hand
from real scientists, and one feels always the hand of
amateur and eclectic sorting, arranging, and coloring
the work of other men. But Hudson was, in the best
sense, a student in research himself, and if his discoveries in wild life have only a modest scientific
value, they are, nevertheless, his own discoveries, and
the literary edifice he erects upon the solid rock of
observation is built with the vigor and originality of
a workman sure of his tools.

All this is unspecific and shall remain so. The
test of its truth is not to be found in such few quotations as the space of this essay might afford, but in a
generous sampling of Hudson. A list of titles is indeed
enough to indicate the origin and drift of his literary
art: "The Naturalist in La Plata," "Nature in Down-
land," "Birds in London," "Birds and Man," "The
Book of a Naturalist." And one should read of the first
sight of flamingoes and of the fires on the pampas in
"Far Away and Long Ago," or consider the remarkable landscapes of "The Purple Land," which are geol-
ogists' and naturalists' landscapes as well as scenes of
literary beauty, by which I mean that it is a scientist
who sees their beauty; or read the English bird studies,
minute and loving. But everything that Hudson
wrote, whether symbolic narrative, specific description,
or interpretation of animal and human nature, is
tinged with science, no matter how much art.

I believe that in this harmony of the scientific and

literary instincts is to be found the cause of the great satisfaction which so many derive from these books of Hudson, which are themselves of the greatest simplicity, often no more than notes by the way. The satisfaction, of course, was first Hudson's. He made a harmony with his environment, both physical and intellectual, which later and more scientific naturalists and other and more ambitious men of letters were not to feel. He found a unity in nature for which Thoreau was always searching in a maze of facts, and which modern specialists have given over utterly. He reconciled in himself the mechanisms of nature and the esthetic spiritual aspirations of man; indeed, it would be more accurate to say that for him they never became irreconcilable. Perhaps when formal philosophy has digested the fruits of modern research it will formulate in categories what I take to be Hudson's inspiration—namely, that fact and feeling are but two aspects of the same world, and that the man who is able both to observe and to express has for himself and for his readers turned matter into spirit.

There are three probable attitudes for an able man trying to open the world's oyster. The utilitarian, by which he seeks to feed his creature instincts, is just now the best advertised. Hudson would have none of it. The commerce of South America has never profited by his books, nor did he, apparently, ever write for a market, although glad to be read. Perhaps this is why a page of his prose makes by comparison the clever journalism of best-selling magazines as flat and colorless as a phonograph. The scientific attitude, twentieth-century model, which leads to the pursuit of facts for the sake of truth about facts, makes better men, and is the chief glory of our civilization. The poetic attitude, where life feeds the loftier emotions, and one is better, or happier, or at least more alive because of a sunset, or the discovery of relativity, or sorrow, or success, is permanent in human nature and not so rare as the newspapers would make us think. Hudson belonged, as I have said, in both of these latter categories; or, perhaps more truly, between them. His effort as a scientist is gone, like the ambitions of his nineteenth century progenitors, and we shall have to wait for another generation to give us more than comfort, efficiency, and an increased population from applied science. Yet in the midst of a noisy industrialism he kept a cheery confidence in nature as a companion rather than as a slave, and seeing what we have done with our environment continued, nevertheless, to exult and to prophesy.

Hudson's most enduring work is probably to be found in that long series of essays and sketches which might fittingly be called the notes of a lifetime. Here is his most beautiful prose. But the urge behind the man, and especially the ruling desire which gives a distinctive quality to his books, is clearer in his two attempts at symbolic narrative.

"The Crystal Age" is not very well known, but will repay reading. It is a story of Utopia, of Lilliput—that kind of a book, yet Hudson far more resembles the novelist of science, H. G. Wells, than Butler or Swift. "The Crystal Age" is a projection into the future which Hudson imagines as a renaissance of civilization long after the stupid rivalries of industrialism have nearly depopulated the earth. He takes the family as the unit of his new order (curious for an old rover to do this!) and it is a bee family, where breeding is entrusted to a venerated queen mother, and love with the sex element sublimated is spread, with less color but a greater average intensity, through a family group living in Utopian surroundings. Hudson, the nature lover, desires a home where there is no sex war yet infinite companionship, a community where even the animals are intelligent. Hudson the poet imagines a dwelling place as lovely as unspoiled nature, and as unlike as possible to industrial London. Hudson the scientist wishes that men might borrow a little sociology from the bee and learn the science of living from their own monkey history.

"Green Mansions" is a better known story, for here the author touches romance, and there is adventure and pathos. One remembers the vast tree of the bird woman, towering above the Guiana forest, the brutalized Indians, and the strange, ethereal creature the hero finds in the forest, a woman of a lost race whose quality is a perfect adaptation, physical and spiritual, to her natural environment. It is a charming story, but it is more than a story, for it is made of Hudson's romantic dream of what the human race might become if its evolution followed the desires of a nature lover.

Rima is the vision of just such a romantic scientist as those early days of the enthusiastic last century gave birth and power to. You will find another of her species in a story told in the sixties by a fanciful journalist, "The Diamond Lens," of Fitz-James O'Brien. But Hudson's nature fairy is far more deeply imagined. She is a creature of such hope as the friends of Tennyson must have cherished when they talked the good talk of which "Locksley Hall" was born.

But instead of a lovelier race we got the black country, the Ford, the signboard, forest devastation, city ugliness, industrialism! Ah, but that is in "Green Mansions" also! The savages that hate the bird woman in her dress of cobwebs because she is beautiful and strange seem so powerless to hurt her until at last they destroy her tree world and her by fire. That is clear enough in its implications. Romantic dreams never come true.

But Hudson did not demand that they should come true. The romance of science was annihilated, yet the poetry of it remained, and that was his solace. His prose is contented prose, with a peace in its beauty. It is modern prose, too, in spite of the umbilical cord which unites it to the far away mid-nineteenth century. The rhetorical swing, the preaching rhythm, of Carlyle and Ruskin is gone. A scientist's cool eye and the observation which is his usual subject matter have given him simplicity, a beauty of plainness that journalists may envy while men of letters admire. It is unadorned prose that yet is beautiful, as most modern prose emphatically is not.

Few men have lived to be a classic, but that was Hudson's good fortune. It was a just reward for a lifetime of happy obscurity. We will not say that he was as great as Wordsworth or Darwin or that he was as profound as Emerson or as persuasive as Charles Lamb. He is not the man for comparisons, nor will it ever become fashionable to write essays on his name. I doubt if he is imitated, perhaps because in his vein he is inimitable, as are all those who write only of what they see, feel, think. But, like other honest classics, Izaak Walton or White of Selborne, or Thoreau, he will always have friends, always new friends who are discovering his calm felicities, and old friends who come back when they are weary of sparkle, clatter, and clash. Of science and literature he was a much-loved child.

A Man of Letters

Woodrow Wilson was a man of letters before he was a statesman; if he had not been a man of letters he might have been President of the United States, but he would never have been the world leader that he became.

Greatness is not so poor as to succeed by one gift only, but Wilson's lucky penny was unquestionably his power to express. The great Presidents of the United States have been fortunate in their ability to speak their minds. Washington was inexpressive except when angry, but Jefferson and Cleveland, and much more Lincoln and Roosevelt and Woodrow Wilson, could make words do what men do, save or destroy, condemn or uplift.

Theodore Roosevelt's literary power was dramatic. His biting phrases made the national tendencies which he praised or deplored seem part of every man's experience. "Muck raking" and "the strenuous life" worked in the popular imagination from the moment he gave them currency. Roosevelt phrased his own temperament, but Wilson gave final and resounding expression to widespread though unformulated thinking at a time when the public mind was seething.

The hot-headed made fun of his war of notes and his constant messages, and yet it is clear now that the

Wilsonian phrase was often stronger than battalions, that in plain truth it created battalions, made America ready for war, gave an army its morale, and hastened the end of the conflict. The same phrases dogmatically uttered by a mere man of letters would have lacked the context of a rich and resourceful country and, later, three million men in arms; but even so they would have had power, for they expressed with uncanny accuracy, first, the ideas of men who put no trust in war; then, the ideals of a nation that wished to fight finely; last, the passionate desires of the war weary who believed that a new world order had been earned. Even when such phrases as "too proud to fight" and "peace without victory" got angry reactions, it was because they summed up beliefs felt to be dangerous because they were known to be popular with many and earnestly held.

Wilson's literary power was a dangerous talent. If it was a main factor in his moral influence, at one time the greatest in the world, it was perhaps chiefly responsible for his alleged failure. He was not a novelist to follow the defects as well as the potentialities of character; nor a dramatist to point out the tragedy of human aspirations (of which he was of course well aware); nor an essayist to analyze the plus and minus of human endeavor. His duty, as he saw it, was to state and restate what men should do, what good men would do if they could. It was a duty which his idealism made easy and grateful. But, like Pharaoh, he would not let his people go, like the Hebrew prophets, he would permit no concern except with the highest, like every great man of letters, he never was at a loss for effective words. We were overstimulated to virtue; we were told too often of the ideals we must keep. The natural man, as Wilson's father would have said, became uneasy. He could not breathe such air so long. He grew irritable. When Wilson called for a moral uprising it did not come. His enemies were more active than his friends. The moral nerve of the nation no longer thrilled.

Wilson counted too much upon his power over words. The quick response of the democracy when he expressed their dim hopes made him overconfident. He followed the natural course of the man of letters, which is to think out the word in loneliness, and more and more forsook the policy of statesmen, which is to work with and through able men. If a general could speak direct to his soldiers he would have little need of officers. That was Wilson's idea. It was remarkably successful until he reached Paris; it was more successful there than is commonly believed, but the Senate was too much for it. The Senate is neither democratic nor literary, and has no dim, idealistic hopes.

That Wilson failed is too readily assumed. It is not probable that he died believing himself a failure, and it is not improbable that his ideas will achieve a final success. He failed to get us into the League; but then we were certainly not ready to go into the League in 1919. He failed to settle Europe; but Europe did not want to be settled by his way in 1919, and it is just beginning to admit that in many respects he was right and the nationalists wrong. He did not end war—of course, he never expected that far-off consummation in his time—but, thanks to him, ideas of morality among nations, of common agreement to prevent needless conflict, and of a solidarity of interest in the civilized world have entered practical politics and can enlist at any moment powerful and intelligent support.

His ideas live on, and many of his phrases will come back white hot when we pass from the moral lassitude of this decade into some new crisis. It will not be by his achievements in national welfare, nor by his services in unifying the country for war, nor even by his incredible energy as war President that Woodrow Wilson will appeal to the future. He will appear rather as a man of letters, fortunate in his opportunity, who was able to start ideas upon their course and so achieve an influence beyond his life and country.

Mr. Wells in Utopia

WISH literature is the happy, dreaming land of millions of good Americans. It is made of that drug by which we put ourselves to sleep at night, dreaming of easy money or romance or both. Legacies, luck, coincidence, recognition, fortunate meetings, and happy discovery are its commonplaces; pathos and sacrifice are its variants through which our moral impulses are vicariously assuaged. The news-stands are crowded with magazines whose titles might all be "Wish."

But the strong-minded can wish as heartily as the sentimental. They can wish to make science and reason prevail as the Puritans wished the will of God to prevail. They can wish for cities made fit to live in, customs that do not cramp the spirit, morals adapted to our advance in knowledge, laws designed to protect not property but men. Usually each one wishes for the kind of Utopia that would particularly suit his temperament.

This literature of the Utopian wish reappears whenever science or religion outruns civilization. Bernard Shaw is a great wisher who began by attacking society as it was and is ending with glimpses of a new world. H. G. Wells has turned sheer Utopian. His books, "Men Like Gods" and "The Dream," seem at first to

be attempts to plan a community where you can have
as many love affairs as you need without ignorant in-
terference by society, but, of course, that is just a
malicious way of saying that Mr. Wells is wishing for
new and more harmonious relationships in the human
race, with less jealousy, pettiness, stupidity, and waste.
He wishes such a society and so he makes a book about
it.   So does Mr. Galsworthy, so does Mr. Barrie, so,
in his brusque fashion, does Mr. Arnold Bennett.

The Americans are not such ardent Utopians.   Perhaps America is altering so fast that it hardly seems
worth while to suggest Utopias for its consideration.
When men and women are trying something new every
month anyway it is hard to interest them in a Life of
Reason, one requirement for which would be to stop
moving in order to think.

Americans, when they write wish literature, prefer
the sentimental variety, which makes them happy and
does not bother about the race.   Serious minded, dis-
illusioned, sensitive Americans write not wish but
wish-*not* literature.   The so-called (and rightly) literature of the Middle West—Masters's bitter epitaphs,
Sinclair Lewis's studies in mediocrity, Edna Ferber's
protests against ugliness, Zona Gale's satires on the
petty and mean—is wish-not literature.   The authors
prefer not to coddle themselves with illusions of heroic
business, virtuous beauty, and million-dollar happiness.
They are moved not by dreams but by pinching realities.   It is what they do not like in their environment
which moves them to write.   And one gets an impres-

sion of fiercely negative people who want to smash their world to bits before they begin to think of their hearts' desire.

It is probable that the roots of the difference go down into the very subsoil of human experience itself. Most of us will always deny realities whenever and wherever we do not care to face them, and certainly many of us are right. Hope, which is oftener than not an illusion, is one of man's great gifts, as the Greeks acknowledged long before us, and one of the prime stuffs of literature.

And the creating of Utopias is endlessly interesting —more interesting to-day than ever, since any writer versed in social science and psychology can construct a logically possible world as full of surprises in its human relationships as the mechanical worlds of the future with their realizations of physics and chemistry carried on to complete control. Endlessly interesting, too, because the shrewdest of prophets, like Mr. Wells himself, cannot be sure that human nature in general will wish what he wishes and believes can be accomplished by willing. As has been hinted before, Mr. Wells's dream worlds sometimes tell more about Mr. Wells than of Utopia.

There is less of that "constructive thinking" which just now is so popular, but more vigor, in the literature of "wish not." One feels that when the Middle Westerners have told all, when they have freely said how very horrid it is to grow up in the Middle West, why then, in place of building wished-for Utopias, some returning affection for muddy prairie and dull Main Streets may bring them to studies which are neither of wish nor wish not, but of things as they are. And not realism either in its sordid sense, but reality, which is a very different matter.

VI

Various Reflections

The Drug of Reading

WHEN the Prohibitionists have settled alcohol finally and disposed of tobacco, they should pounce upon the reading habit, for reading can be a drug. Observe men and women and even children upon any train or car. See how heads nod in a dull intoxication over magazines and newspapers. The man across the aisle lifts his eyes. They roll for a moment in a stupid vacancy, as some thought stirs feebly in his fuddled brain; then he drops his sight again into his intoxicant and drowns reflection in meaningless reading which he forgets as fast as he reads. Human beings, seemingly educated and apparently intelligent, will commit absurdities rather than sit still without something to read. They will pick old papers out of the dust and look at the comic strips, they will stretch across a neighbor's shoulder, they will carry a battered roll of newsprint bulged in an outside pocket, they will read the "Lost and Found" ads or Aunt Molly's Hints on Canning, or the end of a story in the last torn half of "The Saturday Evening Post." In the old melodrama the hero used to cry: "Oh, God, let me not think!" That is what we all cry now when there is any opportunity for thinking; and instead of "Give me liquor!" raise one universal prayer for a page with print on it. The profoundest scholar, he whose picture appears in medieval manuscripts surrounded by rumpled tomes and barred away from the noises of day, read no more words in twenty-four hours than many traveling men who could not tell you by evening what it was they had read.

Perhaps if Prohibitionists had more carefully considered the how and the why and the who of taking alcohol the Eighteenth Amendment would have been deferred or modified; and we are far from proposing a Twentieth against reading—even the three-quarters of all available reading which is worthless in substance, cheap and vulgar in form. For the real question is, What would the mind be doing if it were not drugged by reading? The stolid vacancy of the peasant brain is not to be commended as a virtue, except by comparison with ignoble thinking. The gross unintelligence of primitive man, soil-bound and work-bound, is not even picturesque, and the romancers that praise the happy, happy medieval whose brain was uncorrupted by machine-made ideas, forget the iron tyranny of superstition and convention which bound an intellect shut off from news and free discussion. Vulgarity may be worse than bigotry, but neither is a blessing.

And the answer seems to be that the value of reading depends upon the quality of man's imagination and the nature of his thinking. If his mind vibrates with so slow a rhythm that it scarcely pulsates unless aided, then any reading is better for him than none. The fiction addict cheaply living in the cheap stories of other lives would be scarcely alive at all without his story. The adenoidic errand boy besotted by a page of comics is better off than crouched in a corner staring at nothing. But men and women who possess an interior world of thinking, feeling, living as vivid as the exterior world of circumstance are merely drugging themselves when out of laziness or vicious relaxation they read on and on into the endless padded columns of modern print where the level of what is said lies below the plane of their own intelligences. You can stop mental growth by reading just as you can further it. You can vulgarize taste as readily as improve it. You can get out of the habit of knowing yourself by too much lazy interest in knowing at third or fifth hand what other people are doing and thinking.

It would appear, then, that a new kind of intelligence test might be made from habits in reading. You may test the minimum level of your own intelligence by noting the point at which what you are reading becomes too inane even for your most relaxed mood. That shows how far you can sink. Your saturation point is the moment when your brain ceases to function in the presence of acknowledged excellence. These limits are arbitrary; but every reader should be able to apply the few simple principles laid down here with sufficient accuracy to determine whether he is drugging his mind with reading or stimulating it, whether books and papers for him at any given moment are food or slow poison.

On Reading Fiercely

Too much is said about writing, and not enough of reading. It would seem that whereas only a few can write well and those only when they are prodded until their brains turn over at the proper speed, any one who can spell can read. Not at all. There are 10,000 bad readers for every bad author, and if the number of good readers in proportion to good writers proves to be as much as 500 to one, the Authors' League should give public thanks. For the right kind of reader enters sympathetically into the very purpose of the book he possesses, shares its emotion, and plucks out its thought. He is rare.

Skipping and skimming may be virtues. Not all good books need to be eaten like scallops, a word at a time, as Bacon somewhat differently remarked. But if your brain refuses to follow your author, if your imagination is phlegmatic, if you will not take the trouble to stretch your mind until it can take in a vigorous conception, why, then, who *can* write a book for you that has any width, length, or thickness to it? You are a little wire that will not take a powerful current.

An English critic said recently that the English could not like American novels because the subject matter was unfamiliar and the colloquialisms difficult.

How would Walter Scott have fared at his hands; and what welcome would Hardy, Meredith, Kipling, have received from us if we had been as provincial as this cockney critic? The good reader will always make the effort required to climb up to the edge of a good author's mind and peer into the heart of a book. If a little dialect stops him, if a little thinking stops him, if a society unlike any he has ever known stops him, he is a bad reader.

Some of the literary paragraphers have been getting into trouble with the "period" story. They were puzzled by Mrs. Norris's "Certain People of Importance" and by other books that threw upon the screen vivid pictures of the end of the last century. Why all this description of San Francisco in the '80s and '90s? they say. Who cares what they wore and ate, who knows families now where no one breathes without consent of mother?—get on with the story if there is one, we think nothing of your scene. What an attitude! If the Englishman was provincial, these Americans are barbarous, living in a present with no future or past. There is something impotent and unrealized in the life of such readers; they do not feel living with enough vigor to carry it backward or forward; they cannot carry their own egos into scenes where hundreds like them made a different reality for themselves out of a different environment. Take the story out of their street and they will not follow it. Their minds will not travel and therefore they do not properly read.

We cannot afford such meagerness of the imagina-

tion here in the United States. Not only the past but
the present challenges sympathetic reading. All the
racial minds have come to America and are beginning
to write. Most American stories used to be about New
England or the Far West. Now there are a hundred
way stations. And when a poet from the prairies, a
Jew from the East Side, a Southern ironist, a New
England professor, a naturalized Dutchman, and an
Old New Yorker publish books in one week, the reader
must cultivate elasticity.

This is no exhortation to read everything and like
everything. On the contrary, it is a plea which, if
heeded, will lead to a good deal of much needed damning of overadvertised novelties tolerated because, except by their friends, they are only half read. But
how can you either love or hate a book unless you
grasp somehow the heart of it, tear out its significance,
and make it your own? In the controversial days of
the seventeenth century, when lives hung on a text,
men are described as reading fiercely. That is the way
to read, if the book deserves it. Or if not fiercely, then
with some lighter emotion, awake and keen. Do not
inflict a languid brain upon books that cost time and
labor in the breeding. Put such a mind to sleep, or
take it to the movies.

Cultivate Your Garden

GARDENING is the best, perhaps the only, literary recreation. Tennis and golf, like other games, are debased forms of war and the hunt, short cuts to the active life, or substitutes for it. But gardening as recreation (a very different thing from growing potatoes) has always been an accompaniment to and in its way the symbol of that contemplative life from which literature springs. M. Maurois, in his brilliant story of Shelley's life, "Ariel," now translated, makes the old remark that men like Byron and Shelley wrote fiercely because action was denied them. Gardening for pleasure is the mild outward expression of a constructive spirit. It is like the twitching of the dog who dreams.

There is the breaking of the soil. Our turf is like a man's clenched hands. Roots grip it; the tough native goldenrod and aster thread it through and through; tall, strident weeds send tap roots into the loam beneath; blackberry crawlers fasten hidden arms about a buried boulder. The grass heaves away with a load of dirt clinging. And, shaking the rich loam from his upraised fork, the gardener sees the clear soil beneath and knows that he has conquered nature and is ready to make art—the humble art of lettuce, radishes, beans; the glowing art of poppy, larkspur, and peony; the mysterious art of the sweet pea or the rose—what matter!

Good writing is always a breaking of the soil, clearing away prejudices, pulling up of sour weeds of crooked thinking, stripping the turf so as to get at what is fertile beneath. It would be amusing to carry the simile further. Those bulbs of thought that flower in the sand and wither! The gay fiction annual that has to be planted again every year! Those experimental plants from Russia, France, and Greenwich Village that are always getting winter killed—confound 'em! —is it worth while planting them again? The stocky perennial that keeps coming up and coming up—so easy to grow and so ugly. Scarlet sage that gives a touch of fiery sin to the edge of the suburbanite's concrete walk! And then the good flowers—as honest as they are beautiful! The well-ordered garden! The climbing rose that escapes and is the most beautiful of all!

With such parallels the would-be man of letters, spading in his garden in clear, cool April, feels thoughts sprouting in his mind and rips away with one easy motion the mat of commonplace that kept his ideas dormant. His feet are on the earth, in the moist reality of which he will soon be delving. His will is to make grow both flowers and words. The tractor tearing up an acre while he cultivates his spot does not make him envious. A tractor can make a wheat field or a suburb, but not a garden or one perfect plant. His neighbor sowing seed on dump-made ground, hoping

to raise fruit in a soil of ashes, brickbats, and rusty
tin cans gives him much to reflect upon. The starved
plants that grow in his own lean back area, which
never has been fertilized, caution him. You must put
something in before you can take something out. A
feeble syringa can make that clear. Weeds, cater-
pillars, grubs, flies, worms, confute the modernist who
says, leave nature alone, whatever is real is true, and
whatever is true (even a burdock or a squash bug) is
beautiful. And when his Oriental poppies flame out
by accident next a bed of pink peonies, bad art suddenly reveals itself as worse than a field of honest
cabbages.

The trouble with literary criticism is that there are
so few good gardeners in it. American novelists, too,
need to cultivate their soil; American poets would
gain by trimming their beds and assorting their colors.
And the cheap, smart folk, whose aim is to please the
greatest number by the easiest way, should be dragged
from their typewriters into a garden and kept there
until they learn the secret of how good things grow.

Branford Hill

BEAUTY is a habit just as ugliness is, or fault-finding, or tobacco. It is a habit that for some reason not yet satisfactorily explained by philosophers nature acquires readily and man does not. Beauty is inherent in the California foothills, New England pasture slopes, Southwestern plains and mesas; beauty is destroyed each hundred yards in American towns.

We lost in the '50s of the last century (and Europe did also) what sense of line and proportion we had inherited, and are but just now laboriously regaining it. In the meantime, cities were piled up in miles of hacked and jagged blocks, and architecture became the art of swearing at your neighbor. Colleges built each new building in a different style and the age of Hamburg-American Gothic and Early Pullman Renaissance came in.

But the country we let alone. There was forest cutting, of course, yet it was easy to rest the eye with the curve of hills or the harmony of oaks or tulip poplars, and the rough farmhouse was part of a natural composition which gained in human interest by brush lots and plowed fields.

The age of automobile, tractor, and mass production is changing all that. If the gorgeously illustrated folders of Western railroads should speak the truth they would tell of mile after devastated mile where the train runs through a scarred desolation swept and reswept by fire until not a mountain retains its old beauty, unless it rises above timber line, and the nearer scenery suggests the horrid country in which Childe Roland journeyed.

And through our pleasant Eastern country the auto routes are drawn like smearing fingers. The fields and hills are accessible now from the very roots of the subway outward, accessible but hardly to be seen. The main roads have drawn the worst of the city after them. Shacks, signs, posters, protect the unaccustomed eye from a too sudden view of beauty. There is a hill above Branford in Connecticut which, when one climbed it on an old dirt road, was famous for its uplift over miles of hazy ridges, with blue sea to the south and village spires and orchards between. Now the perfect concrete road winds between vast pictures of stagey old men lighting cigarettes, enormous automobile tires, and twenty-seven varieties of oil and gasoline described in letters seven feet high. And as one crests the hill and drops down into what was once a delightful valley, every vista has its signboard, and hillside shouts to hillside the immediate necessity of forgetting beauty and buying something to-day!

We are certainly the most patient (and asinine) nation in the world; for, having spent uncounted millions annually to buy us cars in which to escape from city streets, we let advertisers, without tax or hindrance, block our free vision of the very thing we pay to see.

And how can a nation that looks on ugliness hourly expect to develop a sense of beauty in the arts? Modern literature slants constantly toward ugliness. Our most characteristic poetry is harsh, our liveliest prose is discordant; there is almost a *flair* for ugliness in American writing. That is what foreigners say and a good many conservative critics. They are right, although they miss that beauty out of ugliness which high-spirited man will make from his defeats, the beauty of good poetic realism, the beauty of the sky-scraper. Nevertheless, they are right. Our sense of beauty is dulled by constant association with drab and commonplace ugliness. We look from a raw suburb to the page of a newspaper, or from a raucous street to a Midwestern novel, or from a sprawling poem to a canned-milk sign set in a thicket of wild roses, and feel a certain consonance. Life is all of a piece after all. The impulse which creates the signboard in its horrid *gaucherie* clicks the typewriter upon flat prose and pushes the pencil through the worser comics.

Far from despairing of American literature, I have always been almost absurdly hopeful, and indeed there is argument enough in the casual beauty of New York growing out of confusion, strong towers rising like flowers upon a dump, or the charm of the American country house and gardened parks. Yet let us lay down as a general proposition that the water of excellence is not likely to rise much above its level, and that so long as we contrive ugliness in our environment we are not likely to encourage beauty in literature. As billboards go down sonnets will go up! When we are willing to protect the country we shall probably be eager to read about it in prose that is beautiful as well as honest. When the essential ugliness of the American city begins to really distress us, the price of beauty may go higher in American print. Literature mirrors its world. But what a world, esthetically speaking, we are giving it to mirror! A poet would be far better off in Dante's Hell than in Harlem, and a trip from Philadelphia to New York by train or auto is enough to make a Russian realist turn to romance.

The Tragic Muse

CAN no one now write tragedy? Praisers of the past
would have us believe that the Greeks were swollen
with great emotions requiring discharge and that the
daily lives of the Elizabethans were touched with greatness. This is romance, and belongs upon the same
shelf with the idea that the Pilgrims and the Puritans
wore one and all cast-iron countenances and talked
exclusively of God and the devil. Nevertheless, the
Greeks and the Elizabethans wrote tragedies in which
man saw his feeble race exalted in pain or in defeat,
and we cannot.

In order to lift a story into tragedy it is essential
that the struggle of mind against mind or mind against
environment should not be merely personal or im-
personal. It is easy to see how the modern realist
would tell the story of the *Choephoræ* of Æschylus,
which Gilbert Murray has translated. A son returns
to revenge upon his guilty mother and her lover the
murder of his father. Torn two ways, by duty and by
respect and remembered love, he slays his mother and
goes mad. To the modern the story will be a study in
the pathology of brooding and the reactions of the
mother complex. It will be a highly personal account
of individualities. But the Greek tragedy is not im-
personal. It has power not merely to move but also

to exalt us, because, though Orestes may be pathological, his brooding and his wrench of soul are not; they are heroic versions and variants of experiences which the unheroic who live deeply must experience; and if Clytemnestra in the play is a complex, she is also fit to play a resounding part as mother, wife, and lover. To the Greeks man is more interesting than his explanation, and an emotion is valuable not because it arises from a complex or a suppression, but for the qualities of moral or esthetic grandeur which it contains.

Are there then no moral grandeurs in modern life, no transcending examples of suffering lifted into beauty? We know in our hearts that there are instances in plenty. Is our standardized, Ford-using populace too petty minded to see and feel them? The slave populace of Athens was probably standardized also, and it should be possible to find a reasonable approximation for their betters in unstandardized individuals from the modern world. Are there no writers great enough to write tragically? The burden of proof falls upon those who maintain that geniuses were more numerous in the ancient than in the later world.

These suggested differences may each yield a partial answer, but none satisfies. There must be some wider divergence in our way of looking at ourselves and life. Science, of course, is the prime agent, inductive science dating from Bacon and Newton, which, as Haldane says, has made materialists of us all, so that we instinctively search for relations of cause and effect as the chief value of intellectual effort. Two centuries of science have given us a picture of ourselves quite different from the Elizabethan's self-attitude or the Greek's. We think of ourselves not as potential gods, but as powerful animals. We conceive ourselves as concentrations of that matter which resides in rocks, and stones, and trees. Our struggles to rise above the animal, our sharp declines into the beast, our submission with all that lives to the chemistry of death, the physics of pain, and the various pressures of environment, are terrible, pathetic, instructive, but not tragic, because we are not to ourselves tragic figures. Interest resides in the process, in what happens and why, not in the tragic elevation which with the Greeks and Elizabethans was the final answer.

A new philosophy, taking into account relativity, may change our self-portraiture. If uncertainty spreads as to the nature of matter and the absolute value of cause and effect relations, the interest in the obscurer cogs and wheels of the mind may shift to the machine itself. Dostoevski, Ibsen & Co. are no more likely to be patterns for the next era than were Racine and Shakespeare for ours. As a man sees himself, so will he write.

Resist That Impulse

ONLY an editor knows how many people write in the United States. Stories, sonnets, novels, lyrics, plays, essays, scenarios, jokes, interviews, skits, and sketches —if their million envelopes could be made luminous, every mail box would glow, every mail bag shine, and trickling streams of dotted light would be seen to flow in silky lines from every village, town, county to New York. Probably one English speaker in ten at some time feels the irrepressible desire and writes his pages somehow, mails them somewhere. The only difference between this age of machinery and the age of King Charles, when every gentleman fenced and wrote poetry, is that amateurs now are ashamed of their secret solace. They do not confess to writing unless they are successful but sneak off their contributions in the firm's envelope with a private address scratched in on top.

There is no spring tonic to compare with putting words on paper. It cleanses the unpoetical mind of sticky secretions of sentimentality, relieves the fancy of suppressed desires to be rich, beautiful, and happy, discharges the bilious distaste which results from unpleasant habits of the neighbors, clears the blood of clogging memories. And then if it *is* spring, the vigorous beauty of apple blossoms, meadows stirring with flowers, flickers laughing at robins which cheerily reply, and the many voices and gestures of life released and flowing, making the brain sing and the senses throb, all discharge their electric currents into words that no matter how dead have felt the thrill. Even the inarticulate, who flush with emotion because they cannot say their thoughts, may write. It is only inhibition or ignorance of the remedy that prevents any two-legged child of nature, drug clerk or president of a woman's club, from taking to poetry or short stories as to a daily dozen, or bath, or coffee in the morning. As for clerks in bookstores, traffic policemen, night watchmen, sailormen on lookout, tramps in spring, and cross-country truck drivers all the year through, if they do not leak literature it is because the right kind of minds have been kept out of these professions. Reading has its points, but for a really explosive discharge of emotional energy, and for a soul-satisfying relief from the pressure of feeling and thinking too much or too rapidly, writing is the only specific. Carlyle, when he grew old, found that reading did not stimulate him enough; he had to write to be happy. A hundred thousand in America have precociously discovered this truth.

Never resist the impulse to write. It is as unhygienic as to stifle yawning or any other natural function. Dip out your ideas like water from a spring. The spring refills and is clearer, and so with your mind. There is an unhappy set of people who would like to relieve the pang of ideas unexpressed, by writing, but will not because they are afraid of making bad prose or bad verse. This is snobbery, and like all snobs they thwart themselves. The song is more important to the bird than to the hearer. Does the evening thrush sing for you, or even for his mate? He responds to the purple twilight with the silver notes which just then are himself.

Root, hog, or die! Write, man, or be dumb! But why for every satisfaction of emotional surcharge is it necessary to demand the cool morning after of print? Why should they who never record their bathtub songs so yearn to publish their midnight sonnets? The impulse to publish should be resisted as long as possible. The relief of your emotion by writing, unfortunately, does not guarantee that the result will relieve others. The poem is your own child and you love it, but it does not yet, nor probably ever will, belong to all the ages. A livelier emotion, an intenser discipline, and a broader outlook than the common mortal possesses are prerequisites for writing that is good for all as well as good for one. Think once and write; think twice before you burden the mails. Lift up your heart and your pen together, but do not try to publish until you are sure of what you have done.

Statistics

WE like to befuddle ourselves with statistics. It is a pleasant vice that produces cheap thrills and quick conclusions with no after effects that cannot be removed by a fresh dose. To-day, figures from intelligence tests are gulped down without tasting; to-morrow, it will be something else.

These intelligence tests have roused an old hare that has run many a course before, and calls himself "How to Prepare for Success in Life." It seems that statistics prove that the really successful men did only indifferently well in their universities; the studious and proficient have not been such good "providers" twenty years after.

If statistics were valuable in a discussion of What Is Success in Life, several remarks might here be pertinent. As, for example, Are the degrees of doing well in college really tested by a marking system in which dull men can admittedly excel? Is there any real relation between a university training and that inherent shrewdness which is one of the prime factors of financial success? It is probably true that as many boys have been kept from becoming millionaires by their college education as have been given a leg-up towards that eminence. What of it, if college gave them what they wanted?

But there is an ancient fallacy that raises its deceitful head above these statistics. There is no means except through personal intimacy or books by which we can tell how others have succeeded in life, and, since books deal heavily in imagination, they cannot be made a basis for statistics.

This question of success is so complex that only literature—and a good deal of literature—can present it fairly. The poorly paid professions, for instance, preaching, teaching, science, and literary literature, cannot reckon their compensations fairly without taking count of gratified pride. Pride will not fill an empty stomach, but it is a good substitute for an overstuffed pocketbook. Statistics cannot estimate pride in a docile congregation or an international reputation, but it is there, waiting to be counted, and scores as high as income or business power.

And how statistics lie about money, since they estimate only its gross absolutes instead of its far more important relatives; such imponderables as the achievement of getting it, the independence it brings, the power that resides in it! Greatest crudity of all, these futile figurings, based upon income or a position in "Who's Who," do not even touch in passing success and failure in the more intimate of human relationships. How delicate these are, how dependent upon minute adjustments in the physiology or the psychology of the situation, scientists are now explaining, although literature knew the facts long before. Indeed, statistics of success are largely negative. They indicate that class A is not badly housed, although, heaven knows! with a million dollars its members may still be uncomfortable; that class B is not underfed, although whether they digest, statistics do not tell us; that the individuals of class C can leave a competence to their children, though what *they* will do with it remains upon the knees of the gods. The mortifications of life, the moral sores and diseases of the will, as well as such blessings as healthy glands, a love of nature, or a taste for reading, are never viewed by these pompous summaries.

"Bartlett's Familiar Quotations" has perhaps five hundred items which express more tersely these familiar ideas, but it is worth adapting them to the present if only to emphasize a new use for good books. If this standardizing process by curves, formulas, and statistics grows upon us, the notion that you can bring up your child, adjust your wife or husband, or plan for the family by millimeter rule or temperamental test is likely to become dangerously generalized. Literature is the corrective, for literature deals with the concrete, which means, when men and women are concerned, with individuals. Put a mathematical study of the effects of sex suppression on one pan of the scales and a good novel of normal family life on the other, and perhaps you will strike a balance. It has often been complained, and with reason, that we who read are likely to make literary judgments, estimating our environment not by the facts, but in terms of what we have read in books. Well, a good poem or novel is a safer guide through those complex difficulties in which the most harmonious family will occasionally be involved than statistics. There is more about Success in Life in Browning, Hardy, Whitman, or Willa Cather than in all the intelligence tests and the deductions therefrom.

Indeed, one reason for the increasing intimacy of modern literature, its plunges into psychology and physiology which so many find objectionable, is defensive. Instinctively our writers are contending against the misleading generalizations of statistics, against the convenience of science, which, quite properly, tries to classify dogs, molecules, women, and emotions in order to set up hypotheses and then move ahead. To think scientifically is what we all must come to, and the sooner the better, but it is the function of literature to prevent us from carrying science beyond its own discoveries. The best interpreter of life for those wise enough to profit by it is, naturally, experience; but literature, especially literature enriched by science, is going to remain the second best.

Are We Educated?

LET us get a bundle of platitudes written down and out of the way and then ask again the question, Are we educated? Education does not mean information. It is not what you know, but what you can do with what you know that makes education. Intelligence is not education; intelligence uses education. Training, whether in the classics or in mining engineering, is only a part of education, not the thing itself. The educated man has learned to relate one field of knowledge to another; he has learned to interpret facts and subdue them to his own uses.

These are not the principles upon which school and university education in the United States was organized during the youth of most of us, and that is why we have to complete our semi-education by reading; that is one reason why the Americans are the hungriest and most undiscriminating readers among civilized nations; it helps to explain the Sunday newspaper, the attack on evolution, super-esthetic poetry and freakish fiction, sentimental novels written for practical people, the election of Mayor Hylan, the defeat of the League of Nations, and "other things too numerous to specify."

School, from the earliest years, was for most of us

a series of subjects taught with little relation to life and less to each other. A child's progress was tested entirely by his ability to figure, spell, or read. Experimental schools in New York and elsewhere and better practice here and there in the public schools are beginning to substitute a real leading onward of the child's mind for a cramming with facts. And at the other end of the process, in the last years of advanced universities, education has come into touch with life and regained internal harmony. But between these extremes is the Great American Desert. Fine spirits are seeking for a trail, but meanwhile thousands of youthful minds parch and grow arid or lose all capacity for intellectual thirst. Some increasingly important fields of human achievement, like geography, are successfully and intelligently taught only to the very young and to the almost mature. Between is vacancy or dead category. The same may be said, with reservations, of the most humane of all studies, literature.

Whatever may happen in the future, the mature American reader of these days has traveled through the desert. He has, to drop that comparison, been introduced to various organizations of knowledge, been taught to work with some of them; but he has been provided with no view of the whole, or of the relation of its parts. Hence, as living is neither a question of reading Shakespeare, translating Latin, solving equations, or applying the principles of economics, but a complex which uses and relates all of these facilities and many more, he has carried his ill-assorted baggage pickaback out into the world, used what came handy and dropped the rest. The physicists said, learn science and be educated; all else is but fluff and ornament; the teachers of English said, learn literature and save yourself from the desolations of science. He, poor fellow, was forced to dine with each and his indigestion is great. For neither physics nor literature alone was education.

And that is why the intelligent American needs wide reading for his education. Specialists have scoffed at this Age of Outlines, not realizing that it was the relating of fact to fact, movement to movement, religion to science, art to morality, cause to effect, which we demi-educated craved from our inmost being. That is why American popular magazines are so curiously informative in character, so packed with articles almost elementary in their content of knowledge, and yet bridging a gap from what I knew of this to what I knew of that which had never been crossed. Upon the casual magazine and the accidental book rests the necessity of consolidating scattered positions. The American who stops reading when he leaves college is usually never educated at all.

Therefore the increasing diversity of publishers' lists, the decline of the best seller which every one read and read nothing else, the increasing interest in the discussion of books, the growing number of scientists, scholars, politicians, engineers, who write for the public, and therefore perforce relate their studies to life as it is lived—all these signs are good ones. The defects of our education drive us, if we are not brain spoiled, to read many books and many kinds of books, and the reading of good books is already reacting upon the character and purpose of American education.

Literature and Universities

SOME reviewers seem never to have read anything written before 1890; and some professors of English seem unaware of the existence of books published since 1850.

It is hard to say which state of mind is the more dangerous. The reviewer without background and standards has been attacked before by me. Teachers of English who are out of touch with the literature of modern life will not necessarily be as superficial and unreliable in their judgments as he has been. The man nourished upon the great books of earlier literature will be able to give a shrewd opinion as to the value of novel productions, provided he understands them. But there will be something very important missing in the relation between his pupils and himself. If there is anything that is continuous, evergrowing or diminishing, alive and sharing the characteristics of life, it is literature. You can seldom or never trace its ultimate beginnings. It has no stops. Ends of periods are inventions of historians and critics for their own convenience, and represent only a very approximate truth. Victorian literature is being produced now. The literature of the late twentieth century is already present in early stages, if we could only identify it. To view, as many (perhaps most) English teachers do, English literature as something to be studied, venerated, and taught, and current literature as something largely vulgar and very confused, to be warned against, patronized, and sampled with caution, is a vicious error. It may be laid down as a sound proposition that the teacher in English or the scholar in English who cannot feel the vital connection, the continuing life flow that runs from "The Rivals" or "The Prologue of the Canterbury Tales" to Harry Leon Wilson and Booth Tarkington, is either atrophied or in some measurable fashion unfit.

All this need not imply that horror of the experienced, and dream of the amateur teacher of English, a university department whose whole energies should be bent upon the study of "live" contemporary literature. Contemporary literature is no more alive than any other, except in an allusiveness to familiar life which rapidly loses its pertinence. The difference between live writing and dead writing is a difference between greatness and its opposite. Chaucer is more alive now than most short stories published yesterday. Swift is more alive than whole numbers of "The Saturday Evening Post." A department of English teaching nothing but its own times in literature would fail, if only because of a lack of standards by which to make order in confusion.

Nevertheless, our departments of English, and especially those of the great universities, should be more soundly organized than at present is usually the case. They should by all means touch by the hands of specialists the historical beginnings of our literature, but they should also touch, by the hands of men competent to do so, the pulse of contemporary literary thought. There should be a professor of Old English in every great department, and there should be a Professor of Modern English in every great department, who is fitted by training, experience, and temperament to reach and understand the literature-in-the-making of his own day. Whether he teaches contemporary literature directly by selection or indirectly by reference is immaterial, although I believe that the latter is the sounder method. Professors of Old English have been hard to find; such professors of Modern English as we describe have only recently begun to be sought, but they are indispensable, and universities have suffered from their lack.

No man can call himself a scholar in English who is not at least sympathetic to its latest manifestations. No department of English is well organized without at least one scholar who is critic and perhaps creator also, and in closest touch with the flow of our own imaginative literary thought. These are conclusions which some American universities and colleges have already learned and put into practice and which all, if they are ready to teach English literature, must accept.

VII

On Criticism

On Criticism

WHAT is the use of criticism? Pope was not the first nor the last to ask that question, and, like others, he damned his profession and then practised it harder than ever. But why criticize, why be so disagreeable as to doubt greatness, why endeavor to set straight the crooked or unravel the tangled? Why not, as some one once said in California, protect the growing mind of literary America from the poison drops of criticism?

It is easy and valuable to write the news of new books, telling what they are, ignoring the bad ones, spreading word of the good ones and avoiding criticism. It is easy to be amiably laudatory or easily cynical and avoid criticism. It is easy to write a vast amount about books without saying anything, which, of course, avoids criticism.

But we cannot dodge the task of honest criticism, in this country particularly, without a loss. Writers need it most of all. Success in the profession of writing can be measured in part by money returns, but success in the art of writing cannot be so judged. The public are quite as likely to buy weakness as strength in literature. Great sales in the past have often meant a great art—and have often meant no art whatsoever, except skill in tickling a current taste. Unless there is somewhere an intelligent critical attitude against which a writer can measure himself, where he can get punches and return them; unless there is a true glass somewhere in which he can see himself as his peers see him—why, one of the chief requirements for good literature is wanting. Writing in a vacuum is almost impossible. Broadcasting to the ether, from which at the best only a confused murmur from millions comes back, is a dangerous business. The author degenerates. Our American short story has degenerated because it has not felt criticism. A literary prose that is distinctively American has been slow in developing because there has been no urge from criticism. The historic romance, which sold by millions in the nineties, bloomed like the desert in spring and then wilted and disappeared. It had a public which loved it and asked for more and more blooms, each just like the last. But no one cultivated it. Roots were not sent down. It died.

We would have weaker writing without good criticism, and weaker reading, too. In this book the drug of reading has been attacked, when people read as men whittle, by habit and to pass the time. That is uncritical reading and it is a poor dividend payer, an inefficient business yielding the smallest returns. Critical reading is human reading, where the emotions are aroused and the mind is awake. It is not pedantic, sententious reading done for duty. To be critical one has to be, first of all, very much alive. The picture of a dry man curling his lips superciliously over a book he is damning is no true portrait of a critic. The critical reader is the human reader.

That, in a way, is the function of a critic, to try to stay awake while some are drowsing over good books, to keep the mind sharp, to keep personality vivid, emotions aroused, judgment active whenever and wherever there is published a good book. And this function of literary criticism is worth continuing, because if honestly and intelligently exercised it is one of the things that help living itself.

Good critics are often wrong, as often as lawyers and engineers; not so often as business men. But a wrong-headed critic like Dr. Johnson may be of the greatest value just because of the intellectual life he awakes in the minds of all but the mentally dead. Good critics are often prejudiced, but a prejudiced critic, like Chesterton for example, carries his bias on his forehead and gains consistency thereby. But if your critic is well read and well thought; if he is intellectually honest; if he has blood in his veins and not ink and water; if he knows this wily old world and likes it without too much trusting; if he has taste and sense, why, he belongs with the poets and novelists and dramatists in the propagation of literature. And if he has imagination also, why, then, we may call him blessed.

The best criticism comes in talk; but America is too big for talking. Hence you who love books should love honest criticism too, and follow it.

Fundamentalism

A DOSE of Fundamentalism is needed for literary criticism. We need an Alexander Pope to declare with fine complacency that Nature and Homer are the same. We need a few of the good old classical dogmatists to assert that any apprehension of literature is impossible without complete scholarship in Latin and Greek. Professor Lane Cooper, instead of writing for colleagues already convinced, should announce to Broadway that no play is to be commended that does not obey the principles laid down in Aristotle's "Poetics." Professor Babbitt should say in terms that would reach the news what he as a classicist thinks of the autobiographical, psychoanalytical novel. There must be some newspaper in New York ready to support a gentleman of the old school who will whittle out a set of principles from Horace or Scaliger and bang modern literature about the ears with it. That was the way they carried on in the eighteenth century, but now we leave vigor and violence to the radicals.

The Fundamentalists in doctrine may or may not be going to establish for all religious men the Virgin birth, resurrection of the body, the descent into Hell, and the literal accuracy of the Scriptures. We think we know the answer, but it is not so important as what they are quite likely to establish for their opponents. If they have vigor enough to push the attack they will force the tolerant liberals, who have been steaming easily on good deeds and pleasant thinking, to find out what they really do believe about religion, to chart a course and put their engines to the test. We do not refer exclusively to pastors and preachers. One difference between Victorian England and our own day is that men who owned responsible minds or held responsible positions—men like Arnold, Clough, Carlyle, Mill, Ruskin, Gladstone—were forced to take a stand and define their principles. It did them no harm, nor religion either. If Mr. Bryan can make the easy-going American take inventory of his beliefs, his principles, and his prejudices, then we shall forgive him his obscurantism.

It is not otherwise in literature. Our tolerance for all kinds of books is spineless. Few call us to account as we ramble among opinions mutually inconsistent. It is possible for a liberal-minded man to talk half his life about books and reading without once formulating a principle that he would fight for. The opposition has been so cloistered, so academic, or so ignorant of the true nature of literature, that critical opinion has dropped self-restraint and got drunk on words. Mr. Mencken, in an otherwise cogent essay, can devote some paragraphs of nonsense to an attack upon an utterly fabulous and non-existent "Anglo-Saxon," who is, if anything, not a racial type, but a state of mind. Our columnists mix religion and radicalism without waiting to see what happens to the brew. The young person erects novelty as a creed and thinks that to demolish Arnold, Tennyson, Kipling, or Dr. van Dyke and Professors Phelps and Sherman is to formulate a program.

What we really need, of course, is sound and pene-trative thinking, leading to principles of literary art which are relevant to that area of literature in which blood runs warmly to-day. Abstract standards are valueless, they are merely rules, unless they touch and are colored by a contemporary apprehension of litera-ture, unless they themselves are a part of contem-porary literature. Such thinking sympathetically guided does not seem to be abundant, and therefore, while expecting it, let us hope for a resurgence of Fundamentalism which will drive us to think. A bigoted attempt, for example, to censor all published books for the benefit of possible readers among four-teen-year-old girls would have an excellent effect upon the fifty-seven varieties of opinion upon sex-in-fiction which are all being uttered at once, and keep a man from thinking. Some of us would have to make up our minds for or against the young girl, and get rea-sons for our belief. And if only, as in the dear old nineteenth century, the Fundamentalists would attack novel reading root and branch, what curious things we should discover as to why we read novels, and what kind we really like! There is a good job wait-ing in literary criticism for what they used to call down South a hard-shell Baptist. He might drive us into making up our minds about many questions that will go deeper than of our own wills we wish to go.

The Ostrich's Head

THERE used to be in one of our universities a course which dealt with what well-known critics had thought about writers who are now well known. The period of the critics was that first third of the nineteenth century when Tennyson and Browning were getting under way and Dickens and Thackeray were in the offing; and the answer seemed pretty generally to be that the well-known critics did not think much of the budding writers and were quite sure that in their period literature had reached its lowest ebb. There were, of course, some prophetic individuals who foresaw the future greatness of the young men; but they seemed fatally to select for praise what proved to be their least enduring work. It was a valuable course for reviewers of contemporary literature. It almost taught them caution, and at least encouraged modesty.

If critics had to be prophets such a revelation of bad guessing would seem to settle their hash. But the person who writes about books is no more bound to long-distance prophecy than the individual who writes about the stock market or the historian who discusses the problem of Europe. What we have to read, or buy, or do *now* is the burning question. The duty of the critic is not, as you might gather from some solemn lecturers, to select from the current avalanche gems for the future, but to guide the public to the best supply of what it most needs. If he is a good critic, the books he praises will be good books, but not necessarily world masterpieces. The early eighteen hundreds needed Byron, and whether Byron is among the greatest of world poets or not has very little to do with their estimate of his importance. Apparently we have needed a strong dose of psychological realism (we are nearly cured) and got it, which proves neither that psychological novels are better than any other kind nor that the critics are wrong in recommending them. A good literary critic must keep one foot in eternity and the other in to-day! No wonder if now and then he slips.

There is an idea of literary criticism very common among readers, especially conservative readers. It is that editors, critics, teachers, and scholars, but most of all critics, are responsible for standards and ideals in literature; that their duty is to uphold the good books, the true and tried writers, the known excellence that has proved itself to be pure gold for any and every time. Well, of course, that is part of their job, and the day when the sun goes down on no one defending Shakespeare or upholding the classics we may justly view with alarm. But it is quite as important that some of them at least should be looking for the new and untried, lest we become like the Byzantines, who had no literature except in the past. It is a very important part of the job of critic to watch and report on the living fringe of books, the growing tissue where the sap is running now. That part of the literary tree may not be the most perfect, but at every present moment it is important, for there *our* life is stirring, and there is the point at which we are living between the future and the past.

The trouble with many worthy conservatives in reading is that they overlook the continuity of literature. "The New Books" has for them an ominous sound, as if *their* literature had suddenly stopped like a family automobile at a trunk line crossing and a brand new collection of freak authors and their outrageous productions gone roaring by. But it is all one procession, and there is never any distinction to be made except getting better or getting worse, and no break in the steady flow. You and I grow older, but the eternal youth of literature will not age to suit our inclinations. Sometimes the old men prevail and for a generation or so change comes decorous and slow; sometimes youth is in fashion, and, as now, freakish experiment collides with innovation. But it is all one process, and the man who damns all contemporary literature—magazines, newspapers, free verse, sex novels, movies, best sellers, everything that has *our* life in it, whether good or bad—is like the Arab who proposed to improve the looks of the ostrich by cutting off its head. If we could keep this head from too much gin and nonsense!—but that is a different aspect of the question.

Football and Criticism

ONE reason why football is more satisfactory than criticism is that there is only one ball. In criticism, too often every one brings his own ball, and when he pushes it over the goal line thinks he has won the game. Mr. Heywood Broun, for example, says that he objects to unmitigated realism, meaning by realism what the French mean by naturalism. That is his ball. A professor in a Midwestern university blasts the realistic tendency of modern sex novels, meaning by realism what some people call honesty and others indecency. That is his ball. And I write in this book of a certain attitude towards life which records things as they seem to be—whether sordid or noble—rather than things as we should like to have them, and call that realism, believing that this is the ball which must be played with if there is going to be a game that gets anywhere.

Another reason for preferring football to literary criticism is that every one can play the same game. Mr. George Moore writes a subtle analysis of the mind of a servant girl as a protest against *fin de siècle* vaporings, and his public, who think they know all about servant girls, quarrel with him for not writing romance. He plays one game, they expect him to play another. Mr. Hardy ponders Mother Earth to learn

226

what she in her moods does to her children, and his
critics ask him why he has not written a story to celebrate the philosophy of optimism. Or, as recently,
Dr. Marks presents the "case" of a pathological family
and is told that life is not so dismal as he makes it out,
and that no book should be written without a sense of
humor.

Of course, life is not so dismal as a pathological
family, nor so tense as the tragedy of Prometheus,
nor so rosy as "The Ladies' Home Journal" conceives
it, nor so humorous as "Merton of the Movies." We
cannot all play the same game when we are writing
about that vague and expansive affair called life.
Some of us are interested in finding what is thrilling or
amusing in it, and should be judged by our success.
And some of us are fascinated by certain aspects
which taken by themselves are not characteristic of
the human animal, but do help to explain him. We
are scientists—anthropologists or sociologists—although we do use the free invention of art to further
our studies. Zola was such a one; Dreiser another.
To say of such work, "This is not art; this is not
typical of life at its fullest," is true enough, but only
begins the discussion. To say what a thing is not, is
no final criticism; nor does saying what it ought to be
settle just what it is. Some of us, again, are neither
mere amusers nor yet scientists trying to dissect out
organs of life to be studied dead. We profess to be
artists, interpreting life as it moves and lives, searching for the significant beauty in it. Judge us then

as artists. But do not ask a butterfly to have a soul, or complain of a "case" that is not art. No one criticizes the criminal records because they are not amusing, nor attacks them for giving an untrue impression of normal life in New York. The comparison is not quite fair, since, if a man proposes to publish a book which contains not facts for reference but invention intended to bring out what he regards as a truth, we are right in asking him to do it well, to be interesting. And we have a right to prefer art to his science, even if he writes well and grippingly. But to insist that he and every one shall play the same game is tyranny, not criticism.

It comes to this, then, that the critic's first job is to name what our writers are doing. This naming is in itself criticism. For example, to describe with accuracy the typical get-rich-quick story, with its affectation of idealism and its surcharge of romance, both palpably concocted to please a gross taste in the American public, is to criticize it by pointing out the difference between what the writers do and what their editors boast of their doing. But, having named, it is time to drop prejudice, such as "I like other methods, other subjects, better," and taking the author on his own terms discuss the success or failure of what he himself has actually set out to accomplish. Naturalism, the pursuit of science by literary methods, seems to us, for the time being, a waste of time. Pure science is more interesting. Pure literature is more stimulating. But if a man sets out to do naturalism, by the laws of naturalism let him be judged. We can deplore his enterprise, but not attack it because it is not conducted like the movies or the novels of Henry James. When the footballists of criticism play the Authors they cannot insist that their opponents all play the same game. Each chooses his own goal; some goals, it is true, are more valuable than others—some, indeed, in our judgment, are not worth the attaining—but credit must be given, nevertheless, to the contestants for the way in which purpose is pursued. The figure of comparison begins to break under the strain of simile—let us say, the criticism should fit the crime.

VIII
Reviews

Miss Cather's "A Lost Lady"

BOOKS with substance to them or endowed with haunting beauty set you thinking of other attempts to grasp the elusive mysteries of living, those dooms and perplexities and surprises which sink deeper and deeper into the consciousness as one grows older. "A Lost Lady," for all its simplicity, has this power. Its story means more on each recall. It is to the eye and perhaps to the first impression the slenderest of Miss Cather's novels; it is also, I think, the most perfect.

A boy tells the story, or at least this history of a Nebraska family which begins in the sunset of pioneer days and continues into the chill dawn of mediocre modernism is seen through his eyes. He is a healthy, sensitive boy, like the hero of "One of Ours," and it is for him that the lady is lost; it is for him that her infinite feminine charm is sullied because it moves like will-o'-the-wisp into regions which disgust him. He cannot reconcile the alliance of loveliness with desire.

The Forrester home was famous in the railroad days of Nebraska. Mr. Forrester, the fine old incorruptible, had been a road builder, and handler of men. Much older than she, lame and retired, he lives on his hill, where old friends come. She welcomes them. The house has atmosphere, a moral dignity, a Cytherean charm. For the boy, Neil, it is civilization and idealism. Mrs. Forrester loves pleasure, loves beauty around her, of which she is a part. She loves men, irresistibly, that is the secret of her charm, and old Forrester knows it. When she is with him she is lovely and loyal. When he is called away she is still lovely, but quickly, ruthlessly, takes a lover. The boy is shattered. Unlike the old man, he cannot understand.

For Mrs. Forrester is Cytherea, inexplicable by moral laws, yet herself a virtue most precious to men. "There could be no negative encounter, however slight, with Mrs. Forrester. If she merely bowed to you, merely looked at you, it contributed to a personal relation. Something about her took hold of one in a flash; one became acutely conscious of her, of her fragility and grace, of her mouth which could say so much without words; of her eyes, lively, laughing, intimate, nearly always a little mocking."

Then comes poverty, then the old man's death. Loyalty no longer held her, even a little. The detestable Ivy Peters comes closer; her own kind being gone, she pursues its crude substitutes in the town, now passed out of its generous pioneering age—"only the stage-hands were left to listen to her. All those who had shared in fine undertakings and bright occasions were gone." And for Neil she is a lost lady. "Beautiful women," he wonders, "whose beauty meant more than it said . . . was their brilliancy always fed by something coarse and concealed? Was that their secret?"

What I am trying to show is that this brief novel

is like a piece of fine Oriental fabric, with a color and texture that catches the interest at once, and then, for reflection, a significance of things deeply and perplexingly human. The story is so firmly and so quietly told that only gradually does it become a plot whose intensity depends not upon the history of a family, but rather upon a mystery of character which is, as with Hawthorne at his best, never quite revealed—the mystery of evil in good, of life fed by corruption, of that quality of beauty which flowers from the senses and can live only when they are fed.

The lady is not lost. From a debased home with a hard lover who casts her aside she escapes to scenes of earlier happiness, and years afterwards Neil comes upon her traces. She had married a kind husband; wealth had given her opportunities for pleasure; she was charming to the end. The story is not tragedy— she had no tragedy; the story is of her, a personality, feminine charm so transcendent that it had to be fed. If the fine could not keep her, then it would be the base. She preferred the fine.

Irene in Galsworthy's "Forsyte Saga" is such an embodiment of Cytherea, but her own inner nature supplies the aliment her qualities need. Her fire is self-fed. Marian Forrester is a subtler study. In her all transmutes to beauty, but her charm, no matter how exquisite, has sensuousness as its base. She will be good if she can, but first she must live, and to live for her is to love and be lovely. Even more striking is the parallel with "The Lost Girl" of D. H. Lawrence, who follows her brutish Italian to the harsh Italian country, where she is satisfied, if not happy, for she required most of all things love. The old incorruptible Forrester, he whose sense of duty was his life, knew that women could be like that, knew that "Maidy" was like that and yet was lovely, and he held her and protected her because he understood. Miss Cather is no more subtle than Lawrence, but she is perhaps wiser in her version of Cytherea.

In sheer art I think that this book is Miss Cather's masterpiece. She has painted broader canvases elsewhere, given greater substance, created a community instead of a character. Here she has been content with a woman's personality, and it is enough.

Mrs. Atherton's "Black Oxen"

The years like great Black Oxen tread the world,
And God the herdsman goads them on behind.

WITH a fine and compelling gesture Mrs. Atherton has challenged in "Black Oxen" two of the most successful novels of recent years. She has been willing, like Hutchinson in "This Freedom," to build a story upon a debatable proposition, and where the Englishman bungled the idea and botched his story, she, from an incredible situation, makes a credible book. With more courage needed, she has chosen New York of the Age of Innocence as the ultimate background of her tale. But here she eludes a dangerous comparison by doing rather brilliantly a later New York, which Mrs. Wharton never knew.

Mme. Zattiany, her heroine, has been a belle of New York when New York had belles; she has lived to the last refinement the life of Vienna when Vienna was Europe epitomized; she has had wealth, position, power, beauty, lovers; she has aged and withered; has worn out her last energies in the War; and then, to renew her strength for the rigors of Austria in collapse, she has been treated by Steinach, her glands invigorated, her body brought back to comparative youth, her beauty completely restored. Only her mind stays old. Living incognito in New York, where she must go to regain her American fortune, chance reveals her identity. There are her old friends, the débutantes of her time, now grandmothers with "high stomachs," bony necks, raucous voices. And there is Mme. Zattiany, Mary Temple that was, *as* she was, to shame them; Mary Temple with a lover again, a brilliant columnist, just thirty-four, who wants to marry her, and whom, incredible to herself, she loves. It is a dramatic situation when she reveals herself to the generation she has deserted; a melodramatic situation when she must tell her young lover that behind her brilliant beauty are the mind and the experiences of a worldly woman of fifty-eight!

Mrs. Atherton has built her keel of controversy and must sail with it. Rejuvenescence through the glands is still experimental. The results of the treatment, the treatment itself, are still uncertain. No one, apparently, knows definitely more than that much that we associate with youth is an affair of the glands. To build a story upon a hypothesis is more risky than to submit one's body to the test, because a story must be probable, and a scientific miracle not generally accepted as proved is not probable, even if it happens to be true. The premise of her story is as dangerous in its way as the controlled experiment in marriage which Mr. Hutchinson invents for his novel. But, granted the premise, the plot is excellent. We have had the war between generations. Well, here is an individual tricking nature and fighting all the generations. Flappers spit and scratch at her. Young women poison her with words. Old women regard her with envy, fear, or disgust.

It must be clear that with a beautiful and most intelligent woman as heroine of this miracle story, the opportunities for situations are many. Mrs. Atherton has gathered all of them. If her novel is based upon an experiment its logic is complete and its conclusion convincing. A green writer would have made a horrid mess of such a plot; Mrs. Atherton is too wise to be sensational; it is not the plot she writes for, but the results of the situation: the affair with Lee Clavering, too intense on both sides to end when he learns the truth, broken only when Mary's old mind pulls away, willy-nilly, from his young one. Most of all she enjoys the new angle from which the writer of such a story can view New York.

Indeed, "Black Oxen" is more than a story of severed ages. This is the drama of the story; but its substance is description. Mary Zattiany is sophisticated Europe. In her new youth she is still sophisticated and is drawn through Lee Clavering away from her own set into the quick, smart society of the journalistically notorious, the wits whose trade is to amuse New York. Mrs. Atherton is an old hand at this sort of thing. She was born a social historian and has made herself a novelist. When it comes to souls and hearts, she is often pedantic and sometimes merely wordy. You cannot describe souls, at least in a novel; they must *be*. But she describes a civilization with an effect of life and ensemble that is brilliant. Hectic, overstrained New York of the super-journalists, trying hourly for effects, sniffing publicity, yet naïve and homely in its pleasures; familiar as a village, yet incredibly sensitive to every wind of doctrine—youth from the small towns baked (not half baked) at incredible speed, with hopeful hearts still pumping beneath cynical brains—all this "Black Oxen" gives us vividly, and, except that the Californian in Mrs. Atherton still romanticizes the New Yorker, truly also. I cannot believe in the Indian war dance in an Adirondack camp (a touch Mary Austin might envy), where her sophisticates drop back to the primitive race they are supposed to be at heart and grunt sincere and melancholy grunts, but I do believe in the broad strokes, the definition of her picture.

The writers of mottoes for slip covers have yielded to criticism. They are becoming restrained; they discriminate, they analyze; modesty, of course, is forbidden them, but they have achieved tact. Yet I cannot agree with the panegyrist of Mrs. Atherton. I do not agree that her talent is for subtle analysis. Skilful she is in her framing of situations and most adroit in her manipulation of scenes. Like Mary Zattiany, her social technique is perfect. But she lacks the sympathy which makes a great novelist, and perhaps for that reason she cannot get that simple utterance which reveals human nature in the rhythm of a phrase or the choice of a word. Her style is the antithesis of the easy strokes, like a swimmer's, each carrying on—of

Mrs. Wharton. She sweeps masses of words before her (some very hard ones!); her characters are explained at length, and in their conversation they do not so much talk as explain each other. When they become, as she becomes, eloquent, her too usual turgidity disappears in a fine vigor of daring description which excites the visual imagination. You see her dinners vibrating with jewel sparks and vindictiveness; her nasty little flappers fairly cavort; and the society of clever ones that she depicts on its tiny stage, shrill and self-centered in vast New York, is as hard and clear as a mosaic. But when her people talk, and especially her protagonists, when they try, not to describe but to express themselves as humans in love or hate or just in conversation, why then Mrs. Atherton is less excellent than many a weaker pen. She is not poignant, not even impressive, in her grasp of the hidden sources of life. It is as a panoramist, an analyst, that she succeeds. This experiment in rejuvenation, this terrible struggle between an old mind's love of power and a young mind's need of love, all these tricks of plot and theme are, for her, just wheels on which to run her story, and, for us, bait to catch our interest, to lure us into the novel. The description is what she writes for and what the good reader will read for. It is as social description, done with a power that beats into shape a turgid style, that one must praise "Black Oxen."

Sherwood Anderson's "Many Marriages"

So I saw in my Dream that the Man began to run; now he had not run far from his own door, but his Wife and children, perceiving it, began to cry after him to return: but the Man put his fingers in his Ears and ran on, crying Life, Life, Eternal Life: so he looked not behind him, but fled towards the middle of the plain.

"MANY MARRIAGES" is a new Pilgrim's Progress in which the pilgrim goes crying for "Life, Life," in a very different sense from that intended by Bunyan. As Christian, breaking out with a lamentable cry, "What shall I do?" renounced his daily occupation, his wife, and his friends, and rushed off upon spiritual adventures, so did the man named John Webster. Voices began to call within him, the burden of his daily experience weighs down upon his life, a "frenzy distemper," like Christian's, comes upon him, and then, even as Christian meets Evangelist, so he looks into the eyes of a woman, sees the spirit alive and vivid within her bodily house, and from that instant is a converted man. It is revealed to him that he has been moving in a world of locked doors, seeing only the walls of people's minds, acting dully, thinking others' thoughts, until his own flame was ready to flicker out. His wife has built a wall about herself, and within it she is little better than dead. His daughter, whose flame of life was scarcely lit, has already begun to lock doors upon it. And John Webster, to whom had come the vision of a world in which humanity's inmost thoughts and sympathies might pass within and without freely along lines of love, is determined to tear open the doors of those nearest him. With the aid of another he saves first himself, and then goes back for those who lived nearest him. His daughter he thinks he saves; but his wife he cannot release. It is she who has stifled him; her soul is dead.

This is the progress of the modern pilgrim from stagnation to eternal life, whose outward story is merely the old tale of a sated husband deserting his family for a new love. Sherwood Anderson, the writer of the story, is a mystic, even as John Bunyan is a mystic. He deals in symbols drawn from the familiar life of the Middle West, even as Bunyan dealt in symbols drawn from the familiar pages of the Bible. The wheel has seemingly turned full circle and brought the modern, with his instinct for sex psychology, back to the earnest "this you must do to be saved" of the great Puritans. For he of Bedford Gaol and he of Winesburg, Ohio, alike believe that only conversion can save us from the body of our living death.

However, the wheel of history never does come full circle, since it never touches again the point at which movement began. Both the incidents and the end of Anderson's story belong to a different world from that society, trembling under the fear of God, that John

Bunyan knew. John Webster is an unheroic sinner in a trivial community, who goes on sprees to Chicago, and is even less sure than Christian of the possibility of salvation. He thinks (as Christian's friends thought of him) that he is a little insane; he thinks that perhaps this new light upon the world which transforms all experience is only a delusion which hides a rather vulgar desire to run away with his secretary to escape a frigid wife and an uninteresting business. And yet the world *is* transformed for him by the mere resolve to carry out this unheroic feat; not a house, not a man that seems to him the same as before he opened the door of his mind. In the fervor of his desire to teach others what he has learned, that nothing can be beautiful that is not loved, that without a free passing of love between minds and bodies there is no real living, he acts seeming insanity. He buys a picture of the Virgin, lights candles before it, strips off his clothes because they are the husk which seemed the real John Webster to his family, and paces thus nightly in his room, knowing that sooner or later his wife and daughter must burst in and, seeing him distraught (as Christian seemed distraught), may be moved to hear and perhaps to understand his revelation. It happens. He talks to his daughter as man to woman, tells her the story of his own marriage tragedy, where suppression of physical love had killed the spirit within it, awakes her life through love, and leaves her with her prostrate mother (soon to die of poison) to go off with Natalie Swartz, who had given him new life, but may not herself suffice to keep him living. For that many marriages (not necessarily of the body) may be requisite.

It is a rather terrible story, sordid in some of its details, almost unbearably literal in more, shocking also, though the mystic fervor of the writer makes a charge of indecency irrelevant. And some of its incidents are comic without intention. Nevertheless, with Anderson, as with Tennyson and Emerson, cities, rivers, houses, streets are veils behind which reality moves. The tale of how in all purity and by accident John Webster met his wife as Adam met Eve, and how shame and lies denied the love that might have come of that meeting, is full of inner significance. More vitally different from Bunyan's prose epic is the vision, the faith, the end of this modern writer's book.

Indeed, the vision of Bunyan is a world away from the vision of Sherwood Anderson, although they are mystics both. The Puritan dreamer's soul was burdened with the need of salvation in a dream world to be gained through ardors, denials, courage, and altruism in this one. Flesh was an enemy. Love of wife, love of children, love of friends, were rivals to the love of God. His pilgrim sought to save himself that by his example all might be saved. His endeavor, selfish at first, was social finally. It embraced Everyman. Anderson knows no division between flesh and spirit that does not parch the one and kill the other. Like Bunyan, he is willing that his pilgrim shall save himself even if he kills his wife, disrupts his home, wrecks his business, and puts dangerous knowledge in the immature mind of his daughter. But it is not salvation elsewhere but life here that he proposes, more life, more love, with the possibility of attaining a freedom of the mind by which loving heart meets loving heart and exchanges life currents unhampered by fear, convention, or false shame; failing that, the freedom of those devil-may-cares of history, the Tristans, whose carriage is upright because they have broken through convention and lived regardless of all but the feeling of life. Better the soul of a libertine, he says, than a soul of earth. Let the whole world die, if it may live again in glory, Bunyan chanted. Anderson would let society as it is go to the devil, but only if it cannot permit free flowering of love and life here and now. Our minds now die before their bodies. If a wife, dead already in mind and emotion, kills herself because her husband leaves her, what is the loss? If a man, escaping the fate of many marriages, finds renewal of youth in another love, who has suffered as much as he has gained? Both conceptions, the Christian and what, for convenience, we may call the pagan, are equally radical, equally removed from current practice. Bunyan's is the more fanatic, the more social, the nobler; Anderson's the more ruthless (he does not pity the lost), the more characteristic of the perplexities of modern experience. We have, in practice, given up the Puritan's program; before we accept the pagan's solution we shall ask for much more experience and much less vagary than is contained in this book. Without further attempt to pass judgment, let the contrast stand between them.

The reader must see from this description that "Many Marriages" is a remarkable book, although there is no intention here to compare it in excellence with such a masterpiece as "Pilgrim's Progress." It is remarkable as mere story, if it is possible to consider the story alone in a book under which flows a broad stream of reverie and mystical interpretation. It is remarkable for its style, which is beautiful in its plainness. It is a style which perfectly reflects its subject and the questing, rather wistful mind of Anderson himself. But it is an uneven novel, disturbing in its incidents, disturbing in its implications, and if the fault is sometimes the reader's, who is not accustomed to such plain speaking, such upflowings, as Anderson would say, from the well of hidden thinking, it is not always his weakness that is offended. There is a defect in taste in Anderson, that taste, whose other name is tact, which phrases the bald incident in harmony with the mind of the expected reader and makes precisely the impression intended, no more and no less. Some parts of this book will be called ugly names, which, as they came from the mind of the author, they emphatically did not deserve. Anderson has done what the anthropologists say man has always been doing, he has taken the facts of love and idealized them, he has taken sex for his theme and transcended sex as we have been accustomed to know it. But he has felt it needful to overemphasize brute fact as if, like his hero, it were necessary that he should go naked into company in order to prove that he is not a stuffed image, but essential man.

In spite of this shortcoming, Sherwood Anderson is feeling and thinking where most of our novelists are observing. He works like D. H. Lawrence in the intricacies of sex, but relates sex to life instead of immersing life in the sex instinct. He may become a greater artist, if not a better writer, provided that he finds his way from life to art. He will shock many of his readers for some time to come, probably until he has ceased to experiment with human nature in the attempt to find its complete explanation. Already his touch, which was heavy, grows lighter, and humor (but not in this book!) begins to correct an excess which came from too much brooding. If we are to have an American Hardy, he is the man.

Boswell's "Johnson"

BOSWELL himself, its editor, Mr. Shorter intimates, would have enjoyed this edition, and he is probably right. There has been a sumptuous care in editing, a nice selection of type, a bringing together of rare illustrations, a luxury of space, all of which the little snob of genius would have appreciated. Nor is the plan by which a wit, a scholar, or a gentleman collector introduces each volume with a Boswellian discussion of his own out of keeping with Boswell's liking for conversation and good company. This is no poor man's edition of Boswell, but at least its format is worthy of the society that appears within.

By comparison with the Memoirs and Lives of the 1920's the eighteenth century society of this marvelous book is almost startlingly different. Perhaps it is only since the War that we can read Boswell with complete detachment. His world contains the germs of almost everything we are and yet in some respects it is as strange as the Old Testament. Boswell, and his club, and the ladies of his story, and London, Scotland, and the Hebrides, which he saw in one plane only, but saw with marvelous sharpness, and Dr. Johnson himself—all these belonged in a world arranged for its inhabitants by the Almighty upon a definite plan. The principles by which they should live were clear to all but the meanest and a few of the most penetrating intelligence. The ardors and excitements of living came from the difficulty of relating them to practice. Being sure of the social order, sure as to the rights of Englishmen, sure as to the elements of religion and the rules of morality, Dr. Johnson and his circle were violently prejudiced in opinion and frequently wrong. But they were wrong in their own strongly felt fashion, not right in some one else's platitudinous way, and often better men wrong than right. Mr. Chesterton, in his introduction to one of the volumes, comments in his usual back-handed fashion very pungently on this very point. He denies that their prejudice was prejudice and asserts that it was principle. The Great Cham of Letters in this and in everything was an epitome of them all and of the best of his age. Rough-tongued, opinionated, dogmatic, he never spared a head if he could reach it and was grieved if his victim ducked. Since all men ought to know how to live and what to think, therefore all men should be willing— nay, eager—to defend their conduct, and especially their opinions. To refuse controversy, to be tolerant of what by argument could be proved inconsistent with principle, was moral and intellectual cowardice. It meant either lack of knowledge or lack of character, and deserved the lash.

The wisdom of Boswell was small; the wisdom of Dr. Johnson was variable. If he said many memorable things of admirable common sense it was not so much because he was wise as because his mind had the steadiness which came from watching the world stream by a rock of belief which never shook beneath his feet. So long as he thought the rock solid, it was solid. His merit, and the outstanding quality of his circle, was character. Even Boswell, despised for his sycophancy, had more real character than many an independent modern. I do not mean, of course, morality, though Johnson at least was moral enough, or piety, but something rocklike in the best of these men and women to which whatever they did was referable for judgment. It was a defect in character which Dr. Johnson thought that Mrs. Thrale's marriage to Piozzi revealed. This is why it shocked as well as hurt him. His estimates of men and women were based on character first and ability afterwards.

The tonic quality of Boswell's "Johnson" to-day is largely due to this fact. We may read it merely for its wit, or its narrative, but we get more than that out of our reading. The book teaches a kind of tolerance in which, in spite of the tolerance of the age, we are singularly lacking. It makes one see that greatness of mind has very little to do with correctness of opinion. We to-day know that Johnson's science was mostly wrong, his theology most debatable, his politics often ridiculous, yet must see that the man's honest attempt to force the world to think as he did was a precedent for sincerity. When he was wrong, he was wrong with his age; when right, his voice still reverberates; but always, as a free spirit, self-controlled, he grips opinion like a man and shakes falsehood out of it. In contrast, the witty Mrs. Asquith is a creature of the films, with no depth or reality to her, but only casual experience; the hero of the modern biographical novel, a lump of putty worked upon by environment.

I am not a mere *laudator temporis acti*. Johnson and Boswell and the rest were still in some respects in the Middle Ages. The firmness of their social order was illusory. Its props rested upon a mass of struggling humanity whose brutish sufferings made the great doctor's own youthful miseries seem light. The unpublished letters of Elizabeth Montague, his frequent hostess and in scholarship the moon to his sun, contain descriptions of the collieries upon which her fortune rested beside which the evils of modern industrialism are trivial. It was a privileged society, a privileged religion, and barbarism began just beyond the stage upon which Boswell's spotlight so brilliantly falls. We are concerned, however, not with gains, but with losses. And a loss in individuality, as well as in character, every page of Boswell demonstrates. We have freed ourselves from much superstition, more false doctrines, and most of that fear of nature which even Johnson, who dared not drink for fear of insanity, shuddered under daily. But in substituting pragmatic experiment for conviction we have lost character with the loss of our certainties. That one loss had to lead to the other I do not assert or believe. The fact, however, remains. Therefore it is the best of medicines to step with Boswell into a different world, where personalities are sharp-edged, and conduct and religion, as well as wit and pleasure, matter immensely, and can make a Johnson tremble with apprehension as often as roar in delighted gusto.

A library, even a shelf of books at a bed's head, is scarcely conceivable without a Boswell. Fortunate is the reader with purse and space who can welcome the spacious volumes of this new edition, with their urbane prefaces preparing the feast. Who reads Boswell gains strength as well as knowledge and delight.

The Correspondence of James Fenimore Cooper

COOPER's fate in biography has been peculiar. Lounsbury's "Life" was an admirable brief study, but no complete narrative of the life of the novelist has ever been written because the necessary materials were unobtainable. Bitter from years of wrangling with a press that he believed always ready to malign him, Cooper expressed the wish that no biography should be published. His daughter, Susan, as dutiful here as she was, apparently, in the disposition of her affections, destroyed what evidence she could get her hands upon, and had "the most interesting of his journals" buried in the grave with her. In these new volumes Mr. Cooper, the editor and her nephew, has printed a brief sketch of her father's earlier life from her pen, a sketch of the as-I-remember variety; with it a rather uninteresting journal of Cooper's for 1848, and, infinitely more important, a mass of letters to and from Cooper, covering fifty-one years, and many of them of very great interest. In the opinion of the editor no real life of Cooper can ever be written even with the assistance of all this hitherto unpublished material. Perhaps; in any case, it is now quite possible to understand his character and account for some of the bitterness of his public experiences.

Cooper lived two lifetimes, sharply diverse. In the first, which ended with his return from Europe in 1833, when he was forty-four, he lived and wrote easily, conducting his life as a rural aristocrat who had married a De Lancey, and then as a distinguished traveler and sojourner who for seven years was at home in Europe, saw good society, was sought after, with an increasing income from his pen and a reputation as broad as two continents. In the second period, which lasted until his death, in 1851, he fought a long battle with the public opinion of his countrymen, lived closely at home in his mansion at Cooperstown, except when he was in New York or Philadelphia selling or printing his books, and mingled only with his old associates of the navy and the families (no *hoi polloi* among them!) which he had known in his youth. In Europe he was a friend of Lafayette and many another person of distinction, and the correspondence that followed him is notable both in signatures and content. At home his circle narrows and narrows. It was the very opposite of the great writer's usual experience.

The explanation is to be found in the letters themselves. Cooper's chief interests were not literary at all; they were social and political. With increasing fame came increasing dogmatism, controversy, and clash with an unsympathetic environment. His age, even his enemies, delighted in his narrative, but disliked his ideas. And his ideas meant far more to Cooper than his art.

I doubt whether the same number of letters from

a literary man exist with so few references to literature. Cooper's books appear in the text constantly, but always as articles of commerce to be sold or subjects for political controversy. The nearest he comes to a literary comment is to say that "The Deerslayer" "has a strong moral and some capital scenes." The topics which we associate with the most famous of his novels—the wilderness and its heroes—scarcely appear at all. If Cooper loved the woods he carefully concealed the fact from his most intimate correspondents. Once, from Europe, he writes that he proposes when he gets home to spend six months out of sight of civilization; but the wish was inspired by irritation with society rather than by love of the wilderness, and was not serious. With his other great topic, the sea, it is different. A dish of naval gossip was always warm for him, and ships and shipmen come into his letters frequently; but not as subjects for fiction, nor in their picturesque aspects. It was the business of the ocean—navy promotions, scandals, trials, condition of ships, sailing records—that interested Cooper. He liked to talk sea "shop," and here as elsewhere he was a man of affairs in temperament rather than a man of letters.

The negative testimony of this "Correspondence," then, is of a Cooper entirely neglectful, if not uninterested, in that profession of literature of which he was an ornament, except in its cash relations. I cannot remember a comment of importance upon contemporary American writers except a few sneers at Irving, of whom he was, I think, jealous, and whom he despised for pulling wires to gain office. This little interest in matters esthetic is undoubtedly responsible for the carelessness in Cooper's own art—his prolixity, his lapses into the unreal and the sentimental, his occasional slovenliness of style.

Positively the testimony is quite as strong. Lafayette, S. F. B. Morse, William Dunlop (the historian of the theater), William Jay, H. N. Cruger, Charles Wilkes—this varied and interesting group, whose letters make these volumes of high value for history, write of affairs in the broad sense, not literature, and Cooper responds in the same vein. The man's intellect turned always towards social criticism or politics.

Are we to conclude, then, following the new school of psychological criticism, that Cooper is another example of American literary genius choked by environment? However it may be elsewhere, such an explanation here is nonsense. Cooper was much more likely to choke others than to be choked. The prime of Cooper's life was spent in cosmopolitan society, and in that prime he was free to live where and how he pleased. His correspondents also are men and women of high cultivation, many of them Europeans, others, like Morse, of European experience. It is conceivable that his beloved wife, with whom he played chess nightly, was not especially interested in literary problems and heard enough of her husband's books while he was writing them to be content with statistics of sales when he was away. But if Cooper had been interested in esthetics, criticism, style—any literary problem whatsoever—he would have written some one about it! It is not probable that his daughter Susan picked out only literary criticism to be burned or go down with her into the grave.

Hence we have the extraordinary phenomenon of a great romancer, producing a shelf of books in his lifetime, of which a number attained the widest international reputation, who did not take his work seriously except as a means of livelihood and reputation. This, I believe, is the exact truth of the situation. Judging from the "Correspondence," Cooper regarded the writing of books as most men regard the making of automobiles or the practice of the law. His first novel was a "stunt," written to prove that he could write as good a novel as Mrs. Opie, with no trouble at all. The same element of play enters into all his subsequent stories. He found he could invent easily and turned his invention upon the American scene. The adventures of Leatherstocking and Chingachgook were amusing puzzles to be worked out and then made into a book. He did not take them seriously enough to mention them in his correspondence. He went to Washington to look over a delegation of Pawnees and Sioux, and then "made up" "The Prairie," precisely as a writer for boys gets an Aztec adventure out of a visit to the Museum of the American Indian and a few hours with Prescott. Cooper, as romancer, wrote with the fancy of a boy.

But the man Cooper was passionately interested in certain ideas, and it is a marriage between these ideas and inventive fancy which gives these books their driving force and their enduring merit. Here again the "Correspondence" is illuminating. It is Leatherstocking and the Indians who have made the wilderness books endure, and Leatherstocking, Chingachgook, and Uncas are inspired by the social and political ideas in which Cooper was passionately interested, for which he fought with pen and lawyer's brief. Cooper was a republican (with a small r) who believed neither in the privilege of feudalism nor the leveling of democracy. He despised a society that did honor to a blockhead because his father was a knight, but his gorge rose against a community that believed one man as good as another because each was a man. It was his misfortune to live precisely in that moment of time when the old republican order in the United States was breaking down into democracy. He saw it beginning in his youth. When he came back from Europe in 1833 the consummation of Jackson's day was approaching. His indignant eyes saw mediocrity, pretension, and corruption everywhere. He told his countrymen what he thought about it in such dogmatic pamphlets as "Home as Found," and those whom the shoe pinched never forgave him.

But this passion for the dignity of excellence, without reference to place or condition, blended harmoniously with the romance of Cooper's books: it gave them a solidity which their adventures alone could

never have made for them. Deerslayer, the man without a cross, who knows more sound philosophy than
the upstarts and vulgarians of civilization, is the in-
carnation of Cooper's belief. The Indians are aspects
of it also. It is not accurate to say that Cooper ro-
manticized the savage in the mood of Rousseau.
Cooper and Rousseau would have been utterly antipa-
thetic. What he does with his Indian is to overemphasize certain barbaric qualities of loyalty, courage,
stoicism, all historic, in order to reflect by contrast
upon the moral cheapness of a vulgar democracy.
This is the passion behind these famous portraits.

So long as Cooper's marvelous invention was in
good working order the results were astonishing. He
invented a marvelous tale and let enough of his passionate dogmatism leak in to give the story fire and
life. But the instant he began consciously to propa-
gandize there was trouble. He was a clumsy propa-
gandist. His esthetic sense, so the "Correspondence"
and his works both indicate, was never very strong;
when his invention was used merely to convey one of
his burning ideas the idea was likely to crash through
the fabric of the story. Readers, like the editor Stone,
who libeled him yet worshiped his invention, were
infuriated by a favorite tale-teller who spanked them
at every climax. In his legal battles against his critics
Cooper was right in his contention for fair criticism.
But he was the first sinner. Having come to amuse,
he remained to taunt and scorn his reader. And since
it was social ideas, not art, which chiefly aroused him,

this opposition, which increased as he became more and more a reformer, kept him in a state of almost permanent indignation.

These excellently edited volumes, with comment on American life too rich to be discussed briefly in this review, contain a picture of Cooper that is complete, but curiously different from the one we had formed from his novels. Here is an honest and pugnacious spirit, with definite ideas as to what a man should be and do, and a determination never to compromise. He is human, too; loves gossip about the right people and passes on scandal to his wife. He is sure of his own position and very much concerned for his country, which decidedly is not taking his advice. But we who know Cooper from his books also must make the addition that somehow this fussy, truculent, most matter-of-fact person had a gift for invention which worked so smoothly as never to have entered into the higher regions of his concern at all and a *flair* for romantic vastness and mystery which he did not allow to interfere with his well ordered life. My own theory is that Cooper's best stories came from the instinctive regions of his mind and were colored by his conscious reason only as I have above described.

The temptation to use this collection of new letters to speculate upon the nature of a great American writer has been irresistible. It should be said, however, that an almost equal interest attaches to the remarkably fresh and full descriptions of the life and ideas of the period which the wide range of letters and writers conveys. These volumes will become a source book for historians, and if the content is too uneven to attain the literary merit of a volume of Walpole or Lowell, yet the interest is cumulative as witness after witness writes of his age. Cooper himself is chatty and fluent; Lafayette, in his quaint English, a self-revealing spirit; Cruger throws light on Southern politics; Wilkes is a new and interesting claimant upon our attention. The "Correspondence" as a whole implies for easy reading an interest in Cooper or in the Europe of the '20s or the United States of the early century, but, granting that, its reception will be as hearty as its value is great.

IX

Literary Geography

The Golden West

As every American knows, the Golden West is California. The Great Open Spaces, where Men are Men, begin where the grass of the Mississippi Valley thins to scrub and sage, and end at the crest of the Sierras. South lies the land of butte and mesa. North, a country of dripping forests, grassy prairies, white peaks, for which the Northwest is too weak a name. Between is the Golden West of California.

San Francisco was born sophisticated, and grew up careless, gay, and rough. Life was easy for the Spanish predecessors, and life has been easy ever since, easy and sometimes cheap. The people of San Francisco Bay are children of the sun, which they court in their architecture and seek tirelessly upon the foothills. They live in the sun when they may, and its warmth melts the New England conscience in their veins and dissolves the phlegm of the Middle West. The Irish stock exalts itself like the eucalyptus in San Francisco. The sea fog, bestirring itself at sunset beyond the Golden Gate, and stretching one lazy arm after the other over the mountains and cities of the bay, keeps the Irish Celtic while the white California sun of noon gives power to their blood. New Englanders learn how to live, in California. The pressure of mere existence, always high for them, relaxes; weather goes by the clock; any day is good for vacation. The land is set in broad masses, picturesque but without detail; brown hills, dimpled with live oaks, sharp rows of eucalyptus, carpets of fruit trees, these combined and compounded make anywhere like everywhere, and all beautiful. Life, likewise, escapes from detail and complexity. Domestic problems sit easily in a land of little cold and abundant food. New Englanders cease to scan their impulses, New Yorkers to drive, Middle Westerners to bustle.

It is the bay of San Francisco that will color the literature of California, in sharp contrasts like its green and purple, its gray fog and bright sunlight. Santa Barbara, San Diego, Carmel are exotic. The East has captured their beauties for literary recreation; writers write in but not of them. Los Angeles is otherwise employed. If it has learned to know itself on Monday, by Friday a new wave of immigration from Iowa or Kansas has submerged the budding personality. But San Francisco, tawdry, beautiful, careless, energetic, absorbs her invaders. Cocky pioneer and tolerant Spaniard gave her the character which she keeps. It is not merely gaiety. A flowing life circle cut into contrasting angles is the figure that suggests itself. Hills change over a week from garish green to golden brown; days are hot in the sun and cool in the shade; dense fog or spotless sky; giant trees or bare slopes; burnt sand or riotous flowers; and also intense conservatism or violent radicalism, exaggerated religiosity or careless skepticism, complete self-sufficiency or jealousy of any merit anywhere in the world beyond California.

And by and through and of all this shall California literature be made. There is no literature of California. What passes as literature there might quite as well have been written in New York. In the newspapers, which contain many features, but little news, the gay energy which is already characteristic displays itself in a smartness beyond New York's. But that is all. The good books out of California are not in any deep-going sense Californian. Bret Harte and Joaquin Miller in this respect, were merely descriptive. Frank Norris could have applied his Russian manner more successfully to Kansas or Nebraska. Mrs. Atherton is national rather than sectional.

California is inexpressive in literature because she has not yet found her soul. It is a common complaint in America. Most of our writers of fiction in particular are merely craftsmen who have no depth of emotion in themselves and no artist's responsibility to beauty and ultimate truth. They narrate and describe, but they cannot rise above their source, nor can they find the soul in others, having never found their own. But in California the soul of a civilization itself is still nebulous. A cheerful light, a whirl of energy, a spectrum of bright, contrasting colors are there, but the star is still in the making.

Yet there will certainly be a literature of—not necessarily about—California. The thing is certain, for there is already a civilization which has very definite and distinguishing characteristics. It will not be an ethical literature like that by which New England in her emotional prime sought out her heart. It will not be a literature of protest like the Middle West's saga of disappointed youth. People are unhappy in California, as elsewhere, but they are seldom disappointed, not often surprised, and have always the climate and the scenery to compensate for any lack of cultural opportunity. It should be Italian in clear brilliancy and Greek in its tolerance; but that is guesswork. Who, in fact, can tell what will be its dominant characteristics until a thrill more spiritual than an earthquake runs round the bay of San Francisco? When the Golden West forgets its climate (as the Greeks did), and lives as deeply as now easily, and breeds creators as readily as boosters, and lets its mind range east of the Sierras and beyond the Golden Gate, in those days a soul may be born. Eugenically speaking, the heredity is promising, and the environment favorable in a high degree.

Mid-West

NEW ENGLAND, austere as Sparta and stony as Scotland, when her yielding time came gave a literature rich in optimism, exuberantly confident of the triumph of the good. New York, that crowded alley of shove, hustle, and push, paved with dollars and skied by office buildings, became the home of a brilliant journalism which has provided a true literature of leisure, where wit has its appraisal and urbanity tempers haste. There are perpetual surprises in American literary history. And now the Mississippi Valley, a land without horizons, where the future has become the present, confirmed in prosperity, dedicated to easy content, has found its esthetic soul, and expressed it in a literature of protest and escape.

For ten years now the Middle West has been declaring through its stronger writers that it dislikes its own youth which was spent too prevailingly on Main Street between the water tower and the Baptist Church. It dislikes its immediate ancestors because they made of Spoon River a place very different from the pioneer's dreams. It dislikes the ugliness of wooden towns and the dirtiness of steel cities which have driven back the forests and marred the prairies. It protests against a certain fatness of spirit which (so these writers declare) has risen by capillary action from the smooth, deep soil into the minds of the generation that were born thereon. Now in several recent books its professed interpreters are attacking its universities for absence of liberality and light. The Middle West longs for something different, but being less sentimental than the Great Open Spaces to the westward is not content with illusion, and being more outspoken as well as further from the world outside than the East, does not conceal its thoughts. Thus from the very heart of what used to be called Philistia, our first deep-going literature of satire is born. Beside the modern novel of life in the Mississippi Valley, or the poems of Masters or Sandburg, Irving's satire is witty play. Beside Vachel Lindsay's lurid escape from Springfield, Illinois, into China or the Congo, Poe is literary romance.

We have never had a national literature that amounted to much, if by national literature one means books in which a self-conscious expression of all Americans found way. Our great nationalistic literature has been sectional, and to this not even Whitman is a complete exception. New England was singularly fortunate in that her rich spiritual life found writers so rooted in her intellectual soil that, whatever they wrote, they had to write of New England. New York has never been so fortunate, although perhaps her time may be at hand. But the Mississippi Valley has found a voice that is not merely the cry of isolated genius and has made us listen. Her most authoritative speech since Mark Twain (who also protested) is a literature of protest.

Logically the next step should be to escape still further into romance. Having protested against the country, the town, and the city and spared no cruel realism in depicting their worser aspects, the mighty valley should give us some vivid imaginings of life as it might be. It was Indiana that took the lead in that abortive romance of sword clashings and shoddy history in the nineties, and we may hope for something finer now. The Middle West of our time has called upon its soul, has looked at its own bitterness, has faced the sourer side of truth and earned the sweeter, which is romance. Nor is it folly to turn for romance to these realists who have satisfied their grudge against a low-spirited environment. The homely realism, the insistent urge toward prose, which one finds even in the poetry most characteristic of the Middle West, is also sectional. Flatness of prospect, a general monotony not untouched by grandeur, such as one finds prevailing from Indiana to outer Nebraska, may have its effect upon style. But that effect is not to be determined from first reactions. If the vast Mississippi plain has led to satire against flatness of spirit, it may also, like the plain of Chartres, become the scene of a determined escape into beauty ennobled by the contrast.

This last is mere speculation; but that the Middle West, like Ireland, like Scotland, like Sussex, like New England, has begun powerfully to mold litera-

ture is not speculation. Such self-expression once begun is not soon foregone. It breeds writers for its
purposes. It makes styles and is made by them. We
are to learn much more in the future of the Mississippi
Valley, and not so much perhaps that is chiefly dismal
or drab. And beyond the Rockies lies another West,
rarer, stranger, tongue-tied, but approaching speech.

The Pacific Northwest

EXISTENCE, says Santayana in that remarkable book, "Skepticism and Animal Faith," is the intoxication of being. We are drunk with the speed of our heartbeats and the impacts of our senses, and we mistake what is happening for reality when it is only illusion. Yet when a man knows that everything that happens is illusion then only does he begin to understand and appreciate life. This is a hard and tricky saying, like many in the book, and the paraphrase does not do justice to Santayana's style, which carries meaning upon it; but hard sayings are good for soft thinking times, and this one sheds light.

Americans had their great period with Cooper and Emerson, Hawthorne, Poe, and Whitman, says D. H. Lawrence in another remarkable book of a very different temper, "Classic American Literature." They lived more intensely then; or at least their writers penetrated to a deeper emotional level and were therefore more alive.

Mr. Lawrence is not the first to observe that those serious novels of Hawthorne, which we called dull in our youth, do seem very much more alive in their own deep-meaning fashion than last year's example of vivid, photographic realism; that Ralph Waldo Emerson is charged with more emotion than Ralph Waldo Trine, and that Poe burns with an uncanny light where soberer moderns only glitter. Is it that they were less intoxicated with the rapidity of being? Were they better able to see and feel and search out the beauty, strength, terror of what they guessed to be illusion and could express therefore by symbol and not by flat imitation?

Certainly there was a pausing time in the '30s and '40s and '50s of our national life when the rush lessened and it was possible to look at the spectacle of human nature as a canoeist looks at trees and hills when, after the rapids, he drops his paddle and drifts with the stream. The physically and nervously restless had swarmed over the hills westward or were sailing the high seas. The dollar madness of the early 1800's was abating. New England in particular had stored up capital and was beginning to relax with the slow decline of prosperity. The fierce Puritan dogmatisms had been tamed by weariness and comfortable living. There was a moment of quiet in which the voices of the spirit could be heard.

It is rash to assert without more evidence than can find place here that other "classic" moments have come in pausing times elsewhere. There is a strong presumption that this has been true, and a historian with chapters at his disposal could successfully argue it. What needs no arguing is that the hour of vision passed quickly in America, churned into violent rhythms by the Civil War and the roaring '70s.

It has not come again. Will it ever come to New

York, to Chicago, to San Francisco? Will their intoxication by life lessen in our time? Not so long as every train brings in boys and girls who believe that they need only experience to make them wise!

A better analogy with old New England is to be found in the Pacific Northwest. There is a country first populated by descendants of New Englanders, where intense activity begins to relax as the boom days come to an end, leaving comfort and achievement behind them. It is a land, like old New England, where intelligent people live in the country. On its borders, up through the valleys of British Columbia, the fjords of Alaska, and on to the great interior of the North a hinterland provides for the too vigorous and gives horizons to the fancy. Emerson used the boundless West as a fillip to an imagination which on each return to the familiar saw eternity in New England. So wild Alaska, when its gold and salmon are gone, will be an *Ultima Thule* for the Northwest, reminding its people that their pleasant civilization is a creature of human fancy and in itself an illusion.

The North Pacific is a grander country than old New England, less beautiful and more magnificent. Its snowy volcanoes lift above picturesqueness, and there is an epical sweep in what is left of its forests. If scenery molds imagination (which has never been proved), the Northwest should have the grand manner, bold and high and, like the details of its vistas, a little monotonous. No such stamping of environment upon the mind is probable; yet it must be harder to be petty in Oregon than in Holland, easier among the purple straits of the Sea of Georgia to view with equanimity the idea that life is a vivid and desirable illusion than in the Black Country of the English Midlands.

The older a civilization the harder it is to pause with the expectation of gain from the pausing. Those who still think they spin the wheel, not those who know they spin with it, can best profit by rest. The moment of vision and detachment will come again, and perhaps in the new world between the Fraser and the Klamath.

On Being Provincial

He that is without provincialism among you, let him first cast a stone.

THE small town in America, so the literary critics say, is the happy home of provincialism. Its inhabitants distrust every feeling not felt on their street, doubt every new thought if it seems novel, and dislike any book not resembling a book they have read before. Every man's mind is dominated by an acute consciousness of his neighbors. And that is one way of being provincial.

But the American city is just as provincial in its own way. When the population goes from fifty to a hundred, to five hundred thousand the pressure of community opinion lessens. There are coteries and clubs, and suburbs, and even professions, in which the intellectually restless can let their minds blaze without calling out the fire department. In fact, the really violent literary radicals get their growth in cities large enough for a symphony orchestra and a Hearst newspaper. But if they escape from Main Street they cannot escape from New York. New York dominates them, an imagined New York of autocratic editors whose fiat means merit and makes success, of publishers who can tell good from bad just by looking, of critics and a public that are never content with the commonplace. Of course, they do not confess all this of New York; in fact, as the cities move westward the adjectives attached to the name of New York become harsher and more plentiful. Nevertheless, New York dominates them, making them force their notes, be smart in their journalism, autobiographical in their novels, supercilious in their attitude towards anything not violently novel on the stage, bizarre in their taste for poetry—all, or certainly half of this, because of the influence of their idea of New York. This certainly is provincialism.

And New York itself breeds provincialism as fast as it produces slum babies and new magazines. If there is a more thoroughly and delightfully provincial spot than Greenwich Village—happily named—let us celebrate it. The workers, as distinguished from the bummers, in Greenwich Village live in acute and familiar consciousness of each other's personality and quite oblivious to the roaring metropolitan world about them. They have a code of social relationships and social attitudes quite the opposite of those sanctified by "The Ladies' Home Journal" and standardized by "The Saturday Evening Post," but as rigorous as the *mores* of a New England village. They live their own intellectual life and affiliate with other Greenwich Villages all over the world, but assume little or no responsibility towards New York and none at all for America.

Outside of bohemia they are ill at ease and sometimes ignorant. Greenwich Village gives youth its fling, but, though glamorous at a distance, its very real independence is down an alley bounded by walls of provincialism.

Yet the most elegant and whole-hearted provincialism of all is to be found in Paris and London. In France the assumption that civilization and France are synonymous terms is an old one; French readers, by and large, are as indifferent to literatures other than their own as to the political and social news of other nations. The English, however, have never been provincial in their politics or their news: the literary provincialism of London and Oxford is from laziness. Where there is a first-rate American book in a given field and a second-rate or outdated British one it is still possible for the best British libraries to possess the second and be ignorant of the first. Many an English critic and many an English scholar still regard the United States as an overgrown dominion. "If so-and-so is an authority, why have we not heard of him at Cambridge? He must be young and presumably very ill-read!" "The poetry of such-and-such departs from the best English standards!" "The prose of this American may be appreciated in the colonies, but its rather bizarre merits will not meet with favor here!" This, of course, is rank provincialism, so tough and ingrained and honest that it has a rare and valuable quality all its own.

In fact, it does not seem possible to escape provincialism by taking trains, or ships, or even by choosing the apparent center of things to be born in. Provincialism is a state of mind. Tennyson, laureate of England, had it; Emerson in Concord did not.

X

The Twentieth Century

Literature in Our Century[1]

THE writer who proposes to sketch the outlines of a period in literary history arbitrarily chosen must accept the realities of his task or be foredoomed to error. Literature was never a simple term and is now less so than ever. This attempt will be limited to books that have powerfully affected the imagination of intelligent readers. Journalism, research, historical study, biography, criticism, will be slighted except in so far as they illustrate prevailing tendencies of the modern mind, or are creative in the literary sense.

Furthermore, time in literary history is relative, even when the dates chosen are absolute. In any given moment at least three phases of literary time exist side by side. There is past time continued and bearing with it the thought and imagination of the last era, in which, in a literary sense, many readers have their only being. Literature for thousands is now still Victorian, notably the literature of the moving pictures and the Western romance in which the mid-nineteenth century, diluted, supplies the thinking and the morality. There is also, of course, present time, especially in the upper currents of contemporary literature which are hurried and ruffled by the events of the day, the

[1] By permission of The Encyclopædia Brittanica Company and reprinted from "These Eventful Years," 1924.

prejudices, emotions, and interests of the moment. Topical literature is in the present tense. And again there is time which, if not literally future, is future in its realization. In this future tense are being written the formative works which will become current literature only when they and the books they influence are read so widely as to become an integral part of civilization. Thus in the discussion of a given group of years, some writers important in the study may have reached their peak a decade earlier, and others be as yet unknown to general fame.

The date 1900 marks, of course, no more than the end of a century; 1880, when the Victorian age began to alter, 1895, 1910, and 1920 are all more significant; but thanks to the relativity of time, any date is more convenient than accurate.

The great Victorian period, which ended in the 'eighties, is still the immediate background of every twentieth-century reader who has reached middle age. It was characterized in literature by abundant good humor and a moral beauty, less harsh than the Puritan age, more elevated, if less subtle, than our own. The great Victorians—Tennyson, Browning, Arnold, Ruskin, Thackeray, Carlyle, Dickens—erected ideals for living as confident and as rich in dignity as the Roman or the Greek. And Victorian literature had also great scope and variety. It was made spacious by the consciousness of scientific discovery, in this sharing a general European movement; and vigorous by a sense of national achievement, also international, although

Great Britain and America led in the expression of
confident energy, with Walt Whitman, Mark Twain,
Thackeray, and Browning. Another vital trait was
the renewed sense of personality, which had lost itself
in Byronic vagueness or in poetic ecstasy in the last
age, but now entered literature again with Dickens
and George Eliot and George Meredith, with Tolstoy
and Dostoevski. The end of the century saw the
decline of this powerful literature, broad but not deep,
more strong than fine, reticent as to sex, even on the
Continent, but abundantly expressive of moral ideas
and all the attributes of character. Character, indeed,
as our fathers used the term, was the quality which
their literature most eminently possessed.

Victorian literature is the background, but not the
foundation, of the literature of the twentieth century.
Our roots, to change the figure, are in the latter decades of that marvelous nineteenth century, and our
writing is fertilized by the dead flowers and broken
stems of the brilliant but futile estheticism of the
'nineties which, ripening too quickly, made way almost
in a night for stronger growth beneath.

In so brief an essay as this it will be necessary to
keep mainly to literature in English, although Russia,
both as an example and as an influence, has been important in the course we have followed, and the 'nineties are almost unintelligible without reference to
France. An observer looking back over the last decades of the nineteenth century must see three marked

and very different drifts of the human spirit in literary art; and as these tides flowed on into our century, they must be recorded.

The noble literature of the great Victorians brought its inevitable reaction and consequence. The moral urge spent itself. The high debate of "In Memoriam" and "Heroes and Hero Worship" over evolution and essential greatness and God, outran the facts it built upon. Liberalism—the freeing of the human spirit to reconsider its nature—began to grow wordy with Ruskin and priggish in the later Tennyson. Men desired to be less cosmic, and went for relief to preciosity in the Pre-Raphaelites, beauty for its own sake in Swinburne, craftsmanship and romance in Stevenson, cleverness in Max Beerbohm and Oscar Wilde, and estheticism generally in Pater, who was spokesman for the cult of art for the individual instead of art for morality, God, and the race. We taste the dregs of this cult still, read its few masterpieces, and profit by its refinements in craftsmanship.

Estheticism reached the masses only in romance, often debased, and especially in that curious cult of the past which captured the United States in the later 'nineties and gave us the modern best seller. The second foundation-stone of our century was harder. It has been called the cult of force, but the literature of moral (not spiritual) manliness is perhaps a fairer title. In written English it gave us one major author, Kipling, whose best work will outlive his cult, and in spoken English the vigorous phrases of a statesman worthy of the Renaissance, Theodore Roosevelt. Viewed over thirty years it is easy to separate the exoticism and real poetry of Kipling, or the romance of Jack London's stories, from their bases of emotional philosophy. The broad tides of liberalism were sweeping shoreward and contracting. Freed and made generous by liberal ideas, made powerful by science, given confidence by the sense of national achievement, the Anglo-Saxon particularly began to capitalize his profits and grasp his responsibilities. Having mastered himself, the Englishman's duty was to show the world that

> Self-reverence, self-knowledge, self-control,
> These three alone lead life to sovereign power.

If the American was less imperialistic, it was because he was still too busy with his India at home to dramatize his conquests successfully, although Frank Norris in "The Octopus" (1901) and Theodore Dreiser in "The Financier" (1912) and "The Titan" (1914) were soon to show critical consciousness of what was happening.

In spite of "The Jungle Books" and "Kim" and "Puck of Pook's Hill," books of myths with a code and a moral as truly as the Greek legends, and despite a long succession of "cave man" stories, and of a side blast of brutal Nietzschian philosophy which seemed to rationalize the force even as it sterilized the stoic morality of Kipling's creed, the cult of manliness was not to be the keystone of our century. Ten years ago we

might have said that the War changed all that—the
War bled force out of us. But it is clear now that in
spite of the wide extension of strong-arm literature into
our day, it was not fundamental and has long ceased to
move the prime intellects in English-speaking countries. It never moved them elsewhere to fine literature, for German imperialism was not, like the English variety, literary and ethical, the Latin countries
and the Slavs were untouched, and the East of Tagore
and later Ghandi, was moved to violent reaction.

No, the dominant literary mood of the new century
which even now is still future in its tense, was realistic,
realistic as the philosophers use the word. Perhaps
the definition in the "Concise Oxford Dictionary" of
1911 expresses the meaning: "the practice of regarding things in their true nature and dealing with them
as they are, freedom from prejudice and convention,
practical views and policy." But we must add to this
the fierce determination to square our conceptions of
life with the discoveries of science that succeeded the
Victorian debates over the first generalizations. We
must enrich it by reference to satire, irony, and literary
realism as means to an end. And we must differentiate
realism in the broad sense from literary realism, an
art term applicable to literary work in periods utterly
different, in other respects, from our own.

Eighteen hundred and eighty, already noted as the
end of Victorianism, is the first of the dominant dates
for the new realism of our century. By 1880, the
great work of the Victorian liberals was done, and the

noble poetry which best expressed it was declining. By 1880, the influence of "Madame Bovary," published twenty-three years earlier, had begun to affect the divagations and careless abundance of English and American novelists, making their critics feel that the facts of life could be more accurately as well as more frankly presented. By 1880, the great anti-romantic novels of Tolstoy were written, with their intimations of spiritual democracy and their implication that our conceptions of greatness and power and freedom needed revision. Dostoevski, little known in English, but soon to be accessible, was to reinforce Tolstoy, and give a new view of the common man as material for literature. By 1880, Ibsen had left cloudy symbolism for hard portraits of the conventions, which he turned inside out. He became slow poison to the romantic decadents. In 1878, Hardy published "The Return of the Native." He was called a pessimist. In the 'eighties, Samuel Butler was at work upon "The Way of all Flesh," a bitter exaggeration of the evils of that cornerstone of our society, the family. And these men and their books became stronger without abatement of their influence until this day.

It was Shaw a decade later who took the subterranean ideas—anti-conventional, realistic, destructive —and wedding them to the new science of sociology, popularized the result by one of the methods most successful in the 'nineties—verbal cleverness. Sentiment was not in his line, and the irony that Anatole France used for a similar project was a weapon too delicate for his slashing humor. Barrie took to sentiment, but if if were not for his charm, which gives him a purely literary value above all tendencies, he would be clearly seen to belong with these philosophic realists.

Meanwhile in America the first great age of literature was long past, and there was an intense activity of material development with only one resounding voice. Walt Whitman is perhaps the chief contribution made by the English-speaking nations to literature current throughout the world in over a century. Like all American writers of real power, as we are now beginning to understand them, he was both ahead of and behind his times. Time in him, as in Hawthorne and Mark Twain, is not merely relative, it is confused, the future and the past of Europe blending in one American present. Byronic in his egoism, Victorian in his optimism, he also was a realist, looking at human nature oftener than at moral ideas, and hungry for facts. His new rhythms, destined to give expression to much in our century which was too disorderly for formal poetry and much not fit for expression at all, were but a symptom of his war on convention. These, and his exaltation of the instincts against the reason, his appeal for the flesh as a companion to the spirit, were all part of what Elton justly calls an attempt to bring reason back from philosophizing in the moral universe to consider facts which had been overlooked.

These men were writing in the future tense even before the strong-arm school had captured the present of the mid-'nineties and while the esthetes were still building the jasper walls of a literary paradise. Great talents, like George Meredith's, that stood a little aside from the road they were opening, have already suffered neglect. Only such perfection of form and complete grounding in a tradition which outlasts all tendencies, as A. E. Housman displayed in "The Shropshire Lad," has saved genius which did not participate in their conquest of a new reality from depreciation. Indeed it is probable that those who, like Hardy or Dostoevski, first presented this new realism in its breadth and depth, are given a higher literary eminence now than the future will award them.

Here, then, are the foundations of our century, which built on for its first decade with no dividing line since 1880, unless 1895, when romance and cleverness began to lose caste in England though not in America, be taken as the moment when the strength of the demand for reality began to be consciously felt.

Those who read the history of literature after 1900, not in critical retrospects, but in the year-by-year summaries of the year-books and bibliographies, will make several observations that lose nothing by the obvious fact that the compilers of these data were often unaware of what their records proved. They will quickly discover a turning-point which for prose may be set about 1910 and for poetry a year or so later. Not that literature violently changed at just these dates— the revolution had been long under way—but that at the end of the first decade change became dominant.

In the early nineteen hundreds, in England, Kipling was the hope of youth with Stevenson as his rival. Strenuous imagination, or jeweled beauty of words, seemed most desirable in prose. Barrie was still a man of pure sentiment, Wells a romancer. Archer was translating Ibsen; but Ibsen even yet was called exotic, Hardy a pessimist, and Shaw a freak. Poetry was in a decline. Books which complained or scoffed, books which dealt with sex, were deplored; books which left India or the South Seas or English high society to mix with labor and dabble in the new social ideas which the Fabians were spreading, did not succeed. Conrad was beginning, unrecognized, Hardy was writing "The Dynasts," Kipling had reached his peak in "Kim."

In the United States, the 'nineties had made the "best seller" a national institution. Some millions of people had acquired enough taste to read books like "Richard Carvel" which were obviously literary, if sweetened and diluted to taste. The wave of historical romance spread well into the nineteen hundreds, and its muddy shore tide still sweeps through the motion pictures. Magazines were being born and were growing with tremendous rapidity. The short story, sentimental like the romance, but more humorous, grew with them. Stephen Crane had made a splendid gesture for realism. The American hunger for print was increasing.

The turn at the end of the first decade began outside of *belles lettres*, but it had been foreshadowed in some respects by the novels of Zola in France. Science and history were weighing upon literature precisely as they had weighed upon it in the mid-nineteenth century. History at the end of that century had become a science, at least in endeavor. It was the age of monographs, which gave way in the nineteen hundreds to the age of coöperative effort. Lord Acton's work bore fruit; the Cambridge histories began, and the American Nation series. History was no longer a story —it was an investigation; and as the field of research broadened, the social and psychological aspects began to be more and more studied. Sociology became the fashionable science as biology had been in the nineteenth century and psychology is to-day. Thoughtful novelists, dramatists, and poets began to see the world from a new angle. It is true that this new view of society was at first intractable for poetry, which in the early years of the century was a decadent echo of the Victorians, beautiful and brief like Stephen Philips' work, or the old lyric flowering in new Irish soil, as with Yeats, or to be found, when sought for, in the strange wrestling rhythms of Hardy. The essay, the drama, and the novel first translated the new social conscience, as they called it then, into art.

A. C. Benson's gentlemanly discourses from a college window represented the essay in those days, a deep declension from Arnold, Ruskin, and Carlyle. The very form was discredited for serious thinking, and Shaw, the prime essayist of our time, chose the prefaces of unacted plays as the vehicle for his social thinking. The plays themselves, when given, proved to be dramatic essays, a new way of broadcasting ideas which had unexpected success.

All this was in the first decade. Now the novel, chosen vehicle of ideas since the latter eighteenth century, came to life. Arnold Bennett with "The Old Wives' Tale" in 1908, H. G. Wells with "Tono-Bungay" in 1909 and "Marriage" in 1912, John Galsworthy with "Fraternity" in 1909, brought the social conscience into widely read literature. This was, of course, a reflection of the sociology in which the generation now coming to full maturity had been trained. It is noteworthy that Shaw had been a professed socialist, Wells had specialized in science, Bennett's formative years were passed in the black belt of the midland counties of England where industrialism had produced its maximum effect. Galsworthy, Oxford trained, and sprung, unlike the others, from the class which had long ruled and thought for England, showed the impact of these new ideas upon the humane spirit of liberalism which had dominated nineteenth-century England and must now adjust itself to a new period or court sterility.

These were the ideas of the new school, but it is as important to note that its purpose was realistic in the sense that its chief energies were used to square literature with what were felt to be the realities of the period. Thus, work as diverse in genre as Shaw's satiric extravaganzas, Bennett's monumental novels of everyday life, Barrie's fantastic comedies surcharged with sentiment, and Wells' narrative tracts all belong in the same category, and carry each in its own fashion the new honesty first proposed by Ibsen, Hardy, and Tolstoy. The power of this new literature is illustrated by the rapidity with which the revival of Victorian sentiment attempted by William De Morgan in "Alice-for-Short" and "Joseph Vance" flourished and died, by the sudden passage of vapid historical romance as a literary form, by the decline of Stevenson's vogue, and the relative oblivion which overtook Kipling while his powers still seemed to be crescent. Western civilization began to seek new realities even before the World War upset all complacency, and literature sometimes followed and sometimes led.

It should be noted in passing how much the stage shared in this evolution. In the 'nineties, the success of "Cyrano de Bergerac" in France, and Maeterlinck's international reputation a little later, seemed to indicate a revival of dramatic romance. Quite the contrary, it was the English not the French stage that had a great revival, and it was the realists, Pinero, Jones, Shaw, Galsworthy, and their many successors, that were the fathers of the extraordinarily vigorous and versatile dramatists who are now making the theater literary again in English-speaking countries.

Poetry lagged behind, and its condition as "magazine verse" or as "filler" was deplorable. Its turning-point in England is best indicated by John Masefield's startling "Everlasting Mercy" in "The English Review" of 1911, a fervid poem, noteworthy for its dogged determination to get at the beauty of the coarse and lowly. At first despised or deplored, Masefield was soon felt, rather than understood, to be in tune with his times. His little "Cargoes," in which the argosy of amethysts and the tramp steamer loaded with cheap tin trays find themselves in an antithesis which is really a harmony, is Shavian in a true sense, and self-explanatory.

And now America, which had contained no poetical movement of high interest, though several remarkable writers, like William Vaughn Moody, since the turn of the century, began a poetical revival which was supposed to spring from Whitman, but was actually a response to the search for new reality. Amy Lowell's experiments in rhythm, in imagery, and in subject-matter, represented the intellectual awakening, which her criticism stimulated. "Sword Blades and Poppy Seed" and "Six French Poets" (1915) are significant. The highly original powers of Robert Frost in "North of Boston" (1914), the sometimes poignant "Spoon River Anthology" (1915), in which Edgar Lee Masters recorded the failures of a supposedly progressive civilization, the homely ballads of Vachel Lindsay, "General Booth enters into Heaven," for example, in 1913— these broke up the American indifference to poetry, made it read and heard again, and gave new life to pure lyricism of more orthodox varieties, by the mere fact that poetry again was in accord with life.

Indeed, "let us take account of facts" became the current motto before the War made us face facts which were not yet suspected. What people were reading, whether in English or other languages, was significant. The pacifist movement, also anti-conventional, had its prose monument in Romain Rolland's "Jean Christophe." Bergson was the popular philosopher because he accepted the mechanistic principle as something not to be scoffed at, but struggled with and overcome by its own weapons. Chekhov and Gorky had followed Tolstoy from Russia, Hauptmann, either in bitter realism or monitory symbolism, crossed the world out of Germany. There were still romantic and sentimental best sellers in America and elsewhere, but critics no longer took them seriously, and about 1910 the yearbooks cease to list their statistics. The great middle class population had begun to read more variously. Its attention had shifted to the more serious literature already available in translations, and also beginning to be produced in original American works.

Side currents, sometimes carrying finer examples of pure literature than the main stream, there were of course. Synge in Ireland was writing his marvelous Anglo-Irish, and like Yeats creating sheer beauty. Maeterlinck was a refuge for esthetics and mystics oppressed by the growing flatness of industrialism. Claudel in France was to succeed him. There were the nationalists, such as Maurice Barrès, the exotics inspired by Loti, the nature writers, also oppressed by industrialism, W. H. Hudson and John Burroughs, the symbolists, such as Henri de Régnier, mystics like

Francis Thompson—but we must keep to the chief tendency; to be too inclusive in a sketch like this is to be merely confusing.

Then came the World War. Its immediate effect upon literature has been inaccurately reported. The year 1914 marks no dividing line in our imagination, and no more than an intensification in the nature of our thinking. If the War has deeply affected literature, the evidence is not yet visible, nor will be until this period of disturbance has run its course. The immediate influence of the War upon pure literature was negative. Authors stopped writing, or stopped writing literature. Young men, like Rupert Brooke, under the stress of urgent experience, became unexpectedly lyrical, and English was enriched by some poems filched from death; but upon prose, and upon literary conceptions of magnitude, the effect was restrictive. Barbusse's striking "Le Feu" of 1916, is now, as we remember it, a brilliant contribution to the psychology of war, but it is doubtful whether it will ever be read as a novel. The War, said Thomas Hardy, was too big for literature. It was also too destructive of literary energy. Except in so far as it violently increased the desire to get at reality, it had little effect on pure literature as far as present indications go.

An immediate effect, however, was a shift of interest from fiction and drama, the popular genres, to history, sociology, biography, and politics. There was a vast popularization of social and political theory, and of science in so far as social interests were involved. Thanks to the importance of the struggle, and the willingness of first-rate minds to write for the public, this popular scholarship was of a rather high order, although it is doubtful whether a single book of first importance resulted. And to this new literature of serious books was quickly added in every language a vast library of experience, remembrance, biography, and opinion which is still collecting; but only occasionally, as in the "Letters" of Walter Hines Page, was there some actual literary merit achieved by the skill and personality of the author. The powerfully phrased idealism of Woodrow Wilson went round the world.

It is, of course, too soon to speak with even tentative assurance of the years from 1918 to 1924. Yet the general course of literature since the War is already clear, and there are several important developments and a few writers of real significance, which demand attention. The main issues are the sudden passion for the correlation of knowledge, the course of so-called expressionism in international art and literature, the influence of psychology, the coming to self-expression of the mid-western heart of the United States, and, most important of all, the rapid increase in the cosmopolitan exchange of all art, but especially literature, throughout the western world.

It was certainly the War which made the outline of knowledge popular, but again, H. G. Wells' "The Outline of History" (1920) and all the other correlations which have followed, such as Wassermann's "The World's Illusion," were a logical result of the progress of knowledge in the previous decades. Specialization had proceeded at such a rate that there were no longer men who could master all, or even much, that was known. The competent scholar knew his own narrow field, and little outside of it. It had become difficult, if not impossible, for the layman to learn what bearing the discoveries in Crete might have upon the history of civilization, or the relation between physics and biology. The intellectual life threatened to disintegrate into a congeries of special investigations. As often, the greatest clerks were not the wisest men, and the application of new science to old human nature and its methods of living, which was a prime objective with the realists, was threatened by the sheer inability to find out what scholarship and science had discovered. The pseudo-science of the Sunday Supplement was being absorbed in place of sound education. It is not surprising that in history a layman rushed in where specialists feared to tread, and that the layman was H. G. Wells, one of the advance guard of the pioneering realists. He was, of course, not the first to attempt to correlate knowledge—educators on both sides of the Atlantic had already begun the task, and historians had given him his material—but he made the gesture which brought our English-speaking world to attention. As history swung from politics to sociology and economics, and began to accumulate great funds of new information, the outline idea in history was particularly valuable. Science lagged behind, and is paying for its stupidity by an outburst of popular intolerance no less dangerous because it repeats prejudices of a dozen earlier centuries.

The search for a new reality which had its beginning in the nineteenth century was by no means confined to history, science, and literature. Before the War it had manifested itself in the fine arts. In painting it led to strange schools determined to escape from the conventional methods of presenting beauty. Of these, the cubists, who attempted to see more truly by seeing in planes, were characteristic and have perhaps been most influential. In music, there was experiment with what had been called discords. In architecture, which felt more responsibility to the immediate needs of humanity, there was developed the steel skyscraper.

The general course of this movement has been indicated in the fiction and poetry which, without being popular in the large sense, came nearest to the will of our most active brains. But literature, especially a literature still powerfully influenced by estheticism, was bound to experiment with technique and subject-matter, especially at a time of change in mood and ideas. It was the relaxation or the breaking down of convention which accompanied the War that favored those researches into the forbidden fields of sex which have been so characteristic, and sometimes so startling, in our own time. Yet the books of D. H. Lawrence in England and of Sherwood Anderson in the United

States much more truly represent a step ahead in the search for reality, of which the War was not the cause. The one a social philosopher with sometimes a golden prose, the other a mystic so interested in the bases of life that nothing, not even occasional incapability, stops him from sounding its mysteries, are both real-ists in the sense of this chapter, with their sex obses-sions only incidental and perhaps inevitable. In a true sense they are expressionists, but that term was coined to fit the writers who, as anti-conventionalism progressed, felt a need for complete expression more urgent than the value of whatever they may have had to express. These threw reticence, and form as the past had known it, to the free air. In so far as this expressionism has brought the sense of new possibili-ties in technique and new fields for expression, it has been a good influence, although there have been no major artists that can be called expressionists. The thing has been international. Werfel, Unruh, Kaiser in Germany, Marcel Proust in France, although ex-perimentalist would be a better name for him than expressionist, the curious mind patterns studied for English novels by Dorothy Richardson, the rather ab-surd playing upon the connotation of words by the ex-patriate American, Gertrude Stein, the vivid and novel imagery of such younger poets as E. E. Cummings, the power of ugliness in Carl Sandburg, most of all that strange, half-mad story of one man's day fully told to the last half-conscious quiver and disgraceful wish —James Joyce's "Ulysses," all are examples. There is no masterpiece of the school, although the influence of the technical method of "Ulysses" is likely to be great, but much of this expressionist work is significant of new energies. A wind of freedom is blowing through literature; a willingness to greet and try to understand the unexpected is increasing in readers of our day. The future tense in current literature—on the stage, in poetry, and in fiction—is deeply concerned with expressiveness and its technique.

Current literature is still more concerned with psychology, and one finds it quite impossible to understand the advanced literature of the last few years without reference to the rapid development of the science of psychology in the past decade. Although the creative artists, precisely as in Darwin's day, imperfectly comprehend the problems at issue for scientists, they well understand that the studies of Freud and Jung have made what used to be called instinct, and is now popularly discussed as the subconsciousness, a factor to be reckoned with in every action. Every vital book now shows intuition reaching out along this new path towards new interpretations. With almost equal readiness, the writers have apprehended the behaviorists' very different discoveries, and are transferring responsibility, in their plays and novels, from the soul to the environment, with suspicious celerity. Much bad science has gone into contemporary literature, but the possibilities of fiction and drama particularly have been definitely and considerably enlarged.

Expressionism was one phase of a movement that included the passionate strivings of scientists to capture the realities of the human machine. The discovery of itself in literature by the Middle West of America was a much simpler phenomenon, but no better illustration could be offered of the drive toward reality worked upon by the nationalistic impulses of the War. New England had become articulate in the first half of the nineteenth century. The West was often described but actually dumb. Frank Norris' attempts at epic interpretation in "The Octopus" and "The Pit" at the turn of the century, Theodore Dreiser's later stories were quite as much American experiments in Zolaism as western self-expression. But with such poetry as "Spoon River Anthology," and such novels as Sinclair Lewis's "Main Street" (1920) and "Babbitt" (1922), there began a real western school very different from the western stuff of movies and cheap magazines.

"Main Street" was an attempt to view critically the distinctively American civilization made in the Middle West, and now seen by Americans who had become race conscious in the War. Miss Willa Cather, in a remarkable series of novels, of which "A Lost Lady" (1923) is perhaps the finest, gives the sudden self-consciousness of interior America without the propaganda of social criticism which Lewis had learned from Wells. Miss Zona Gale's "Miss Lulu Bett" (1920) is another example of the coming of age of a great community, to which that easy humorist, Booth Tarkington, will be seen to have been an important contributor. Books more really important than contemporary English work of the kind, although not necessarily finer, have resulted. When the shadow of Zola, which the two women mentioned have escaped, but which rests upon the men of the Middle West, is lifted, we may expect what we will from this troubled heart of a nation in which the struggle of man with his industrialism is going to be fiercest.

The relative importance of American literature was, indeed, greater in the last years of the period under discussion than at any time since the great New Englanders of the nineteenth century. In the interim, America had contributed only two great names to English literature, Mark Twain and Walt Whitman, with a reservation for Henry James, if he be called American. The difference to-day is marked not by the emergence of first-rate geniuses, but by the vigor of the national literature, which exceeds that of any of the European races. An intense activity in criticism, a versatile acted drama, rich in technique, supplying the London as well as the New York stage, a widely read poetry, and the presence in fiction of a subject-matter more novel and more vital than in contemporary French or British work of equal or greater competence, is evidence of vitality if not of genius. Only the short story, preëminent in the nineteenth century, has been standardized into a dead level of mechanical excellence. A discussion of literary excellence rather than broad tendencies would have to include the fine satiric fiction of

Mrs. Edith Wharton, the intensely intellectual poetry of Edwin Arlington Robinson, the poignant lyrics of Edna St. Vincent Millay, the ironic phantasy of James Branch Cabell, and other items which, like the long and equivalent list of eminent names in other countries and languages, must be omitted from a chapter which deals with direction rather than quality.

Most striking of all these current phenomena, and world-wide in its effects, is the exchange of books, growing yearly more rapid, among all the great literatures. In this, of course, the War was an inciting factor of magnitude, but the barter of ideas and imagination was extensive before and has probably only just begun. Poetry is translated only with difficulty, but fiction and drama and books of fact and opinion (like Papini's "Life of Christ" which became a best seller in America) are now international in the best sense, for without losing the characteristics which race or environment may have given them, they become the literature of other races. The effect has been a perceptible increase in the flexibility of the British and American mind, and presumably of the Continental mind also. The popular success in English of perhaps the most interesting writer of the period, Joseph Conrad, is almost inconceivable in the nineteenth century, certainly in America. In a language that in spite of its gorgeous texture is often unidiomatic, he has written with a Slavic intensity foreign to his adopted literature; and without any of the tricks of popular fiction, has got a reading circle as large as those of the old best sellers. His example is probably too difficult to be followed; but we shall have more and more writers who, like Henry James, write for the cosmopolitan; and more and more authors like Ibáñez, Ibsen, France, Rolland, D'Annunzio, Nexö, Chekhov, Dostoevski, Molnar, Hamsun, Bojer, who have at least two languages in which they are eminent.

Thus the outstanding characteristic of literature at the beginning of the century was a revolt against conventions, especially the conventions of bourgeois liberalism. The outstanding characteristic of important literature throughout the period has been a new search for reality, conducted by satire, by phantasy, by psychological analysis, by literary realism, and, with Conrad, in the very medium of romance. Science, and particularly the science of society and psychology, has been as influential throughout as the classics in the eighteenth century or the philosophy of Rousseau or the theory of evolution later. It is apparently not a literature of great names that we have discussed, although Hardy, Shaw, Anatole France, Conrad, James, give pause, and we are too close to the product to make such an assertion with any conviction. Yet no one can reconsider and compare the books of the early years of the twentieth century with that part of contemporary literature in which the intellectual fire of our day burns and quivers, without realizing that we have crossed from one world to another. The years of the youth of those who came to maturity in the 'nineties are as historical now as the era of "Uncle Tom's Cabin" or the bounding humor and easy acceptance of a confident theory of living in Dickens and Thackeray. Ours is still an age of experiment, perhaps close to its end. Its chief problem is industrialism, its chief question the bearing of powerfully advancing science upon the meaning of life. It is an age in which means have been stressed more than ends. If the search for reality which has been the chief subject of this chapter should reach out toward final objectives, literature would reach with it, and, without loss of vigor or reality, nobility and scope, now lacking (for variety is not breadth), might both come back.